MEDDLING

John Lachs

MEDDLING

ON THE VIRTUE
OF LEAVING OTHERS ALONE

Indiana University Press

BLOOMINGTON & INDIANAPOLIS

This book is a publication of

Indiana University Press
Office of Scholarly Publishing
Herman B Wells Library 350
1320 East 10th Street
Bloomington, Indiana 47405 USA

iupress.indiana.edu

Telephone 800-842-6796
Fax 812-855-7931

Manufactured in the
United States of America

Library of Congress
Cataloging-in-Publication Data

Lachs, John.
    Meddling : on the virtue of
leaving others alone / John Lachs.
    pages cm. — (American
philosophy)
    ISBN 978-0-253-01471-9 (hardcover
: alk. paper) — ISBN 978-0-253-
01476-4 (pbk. : alk. paper) — ISBN
978-0-253-01479-5 (ebook) 1. Conduct
of life. 2. Respect for persons. 3.
Interpersonal relations—Moral
and ethical aspects. 4. Autonomy
(Psychology)—Moral and ethical
aspects. 5. Privacy. I. Title.
    BJ1533.R42L33 2014
    170'.44—dc23
                            2014008352

1 2 3 4 5   19 18 17 16 15 14

To my wife and children, who love without meddling

Contents

MEDDLING

1

APPLES AND PLURALISM

IMAGINE A WORLD in which there is only one sort of fruit, say, apples. There are, of course, several types of apples, including yellow and red delicious, Jonathan, and Granny Smith; occasionally one even encounters a bad apple. The people in this world learn to appreciate apples, eating them raw and baking them, flavoring them, juicing them, turning them into sauce, and making them into filling for wonderful pies. As a result of their cultivation, apples become available in a surprising variety of flavors and as ingredients in a bewildering array of dishes.

What should we say of these apple people? First, that they took advantage of the possibilities of their raw material, creating something fine out of what, left to itself, would be common and boring. Should we feel sorry for them because they were impoverished, never having enjoyed the glory of a pear? Such feelings seem appropriate when we contemplate our good fortune in having a hundred different types of fruit available year round. But if the apple people led impoverished lives, so do we, because we must get by without another hundred fruits whose names we don't know and whose flavors we cannot even imagine. Just as we can say to the apple people that they would be better off if they could get some grapes, so people from a richer planet could lecture us that our lives without their favorite fruit must be sadly hollow.

What we should tell the apple people is that we are impressed with how much they made of what they had. Their attitude is surely right: we must use what is at hand, enhancing it intelligently to make life a little better. Notice that enhancement consists of diversification; humans tend not to be like cats, happy with dry food morning and night. As Gottfried Wilhelm von Leibniz knew, variety is a great good—so great, in fact, that without a measure of it, life becomes unbearable. Sensory deprivation, solitary confinement, and isolation in the dark of polar winter can drive people berserk.

Variety in the form of diverse experiences can make existence satisfying, perhaps even exciting. People generally agree that a world in which there are many different sorts of cuisines is better than one in which we have only goulash to eat. The reason for this is twofold. Different tastes add to the modalities of our satisfaction, enabling us to experience surprising delights. Further, the spread of alternatives gives play to choice, so we can enjoy the satisfactions not only of savoring unforeseen textures and tastes but also of freely deciding what to eat. In such a world one can still eat goulash every day, but only if one so chooses.

Who could take offense at seeing French, Chinese, and Ethiopian restaurants opening their doors side by side? The more the better, I am inclined to say, even though I cannot imagine ever wanting to visit some of them. Normally we are happy to let such harmless competitions play out and consider ourselves fortunate to have a choice of where to eat. Plurality does not bother us in such contexts, and we show a commendable readiness to leave others alone. We are simply indifferent in these matters, and that indifference serves as the condition of others pursuing their goals in their own ways.

Not only do I fail to be bothered by the variety of restaurants in the neighborhood, but I also have little concern about what they do in their kitchens. The secrets of kitchens are like the secrets of bedrooms: sensible people do not want to know how their strange neighbors prepare food or for love. Such wholesome distance makes for good relations, enabling us to enjoy fine meals and our neighbors' satisfied smiles. The resultant relationships permit people to flourish on the basis of their own efforts and the voluntary cooperation of others.

Distressingly, when it comes to some matters, the distance is difficult to keep. Some people cannot abide seeing young men with long hair or earrings; others call the police to stop lovers kissing in the park. Individuals dressed in a way that is generally deemed tasteless or unkempt earn social censure. Those who voice opinions out of favor or choose unconventional courses of life are viewed with suspicion. Bodies that don't meet prevailing standards are thought to be in need of correction, and people whose religious preferences differ from the norm arouse the sense that they are unreliable.

Xenophobia is a comfortable state; it is vastly comforting if everyone looks the same, feels the same, and expresses common sentiments in a shared language. This enables us to exclude the different as abhorrent, morally flawed, or unnatural. If the different should find its way into our midst, we feel entitled to shun it or to stamp it out; surely, it and it alone must be responsible for whatever misfortune befalls the community. Generosity soon comes to consist of saving people from their awful selves; we spare no effort in criticizing, correcting, and converting them. But conversion may be too kind or impossible; women cannot readily be turned into men, nor blacks into whites. As a result, oppression and obliteration appear from time to time as justifiable ways of dealing with minorities of race, religion, and ethnicity.

We can see an important difference between the apple people and many closed communities: the former work to diversify their meager supply of fruit while the latter do everything in their power to limit diversity to a few acceptable forms of the same general type. One is hard put to think of a society that has promoted a plurality of values among its members. On the contrary, by design or unconsciously, communities shape young people and immigrants in their own image, heaping rewards on those who conform and making deviance a source of pain. Even when the United States was wide open to immigration, it thought of itself as a melting pot in which new arrivals would burn off their foreign trappings and, through education in English and in a new way of life, could soon become indistinguishable from the locals.

Why do we gladly diversify our food but avoid the different when it comes to people, values, and behavior? The reasons are many. The unfamiliar is uncomfortable and the strange makes us feel out of place. Seeing people do what for us is taboo may be threatening or, precisely because of its attraction, a source of resentment. Moreover, the different heralds a possible need for change, and even in a society such as ours, given to the veneration of the new, change is kept within narrow limits. In religion, sexual practices, and family life, differences are disquieting and touch the deepest recesses of our being, evoking visceral responses and sundering the world into "them" and "us."

Historically the most powerful factors in developing an antagonistic attitude toward the different have been a desire and a conviction. The desire is to exert power over others and thereby to put our stamp on at least a small portion of the universe. The justifying conviction consists of the claim that our values and our ways of behaving are natural and right. The desire is familiar to all of us, though rarely acknowledged. The conviction seems innocent and therefore unsuspected, yet it structures much of what we think and do.

Controlling others is actually more than a desire; it is a burning urge. Its source may be evolutionary; in this dangerous world, those who can channel the aggressions of others or can at least enlist them to their aid improve their chances of survival. But the drive is generalized and roils behavior long after ordered social life makes the struggle for physical existence unnecessary. Accordingly, parents want to make their children "behave," the police often exercise overweening power, and bureaucrats take delight in forcing everyone to obey their rules. Salespeople want us to buy their goods, solicitors maneuver donors to give more than they wish, and neighbors often seek to impose arbitrary limits on what their neighbors can do with their land.

The desire to exercise power over others is so great that children find it difficult to escape the domination of parents even after they grow up, politicians resist term limits with all of their might, and individuals who built businesses want never to retire. That people seek others to tell them what to do, paying fortunes to hire interior decorators, personal trainers, and consultants of every sort, may appear as evidence against this view. In fact, however, it is further confirmation: in hiring them, they do our bidding. Although we listen to them, we determine what we want, and thus the last word is always ours. They let us wield power over them for a fee.

The conviction that seems to justify our lording it over others is that what we, and people like us, do is natural and right. The customary defines the natural; the food we ate as children has not only the warmth of familiarity but also an astonishing appropriateness. Some think that goulash is a dish invented by

God and that it is only perversity that keeps people from eating it; others believe that the paradigm of food is pasta, lamb kidneys, or the lungs of cows. We tend to feel the same assurance about clothing, table habits, raising children, sexuality, ambition, profit, the treatment of women, the range of acceptable life plans, and religion. We grow into thinking that our tradition articulates the requirements of nature and that we do things exactly as it has ordained. I was raised to believe that God spoke Hungarian, as did everyone else uncorrupted by the misfortune of being born and raised in foreign lands.

I cannot overemphasize the significance and power of this innocent social egocentrism. "Innocent" in this context means the unintentional or unreflective intuitive embrace of a certain way of life, which happens to be the only one offered as a model. Anointing our ways as natural, however, loses its innocence when it begins to serve as the foundation of xenophobia and illusions of grandeur, leading genders, tribes, classes, races, and nations to develop a hierarchy of worthiness, each awarding itself the top spot. That way lies the history of humankind, which has certainly not been an innocent affair, spread out over millennia of injustice and exclusion. The cruelty and the horror of it far exceed what animals do to each other in response to the call of hunger; humans crush one another not as a result of justifiable need, but in the name of establishing the natural order of things.

German philosopher Arthur Schopenhauer saw as clearly as anyone that will seeks to overpower will and that it takes a relatively high level of moral culture to resist getting one's satisfactions that way. His recommendation of universal sympathy as the antidote to this cruel self-seeking, however, goes too far. We have no business cheering on oppressive wills, and in any case it is too much to ask that we invest ourselves in every failing cause. Something much less strenuous and therefore much more doable is adequate to make the world a better place: *we have to learn to leave people alone.* Although this sounds like an endorsement of moral isolation, it is not. Letting others be as a pervasive moral disposition is perfectly compatible with living in a community with them, caring for them, and responding to their needs. All it forbids is uninvited interference in their affairs—that is, making them do what we want, even if we think it is justified by being good for them.

Philosophers have not been excellent at acknowledging the importance of leaving others alone and reducing our obligations to a sensible level. Josiah Royce declared, "There is no rest in Zion": the moral person must be engaged in doing the Lord's work without cease. We must right all wrongs, meet every need, and vanquish the evil that surrounds us. We are familiar with the hyperventilation to which this gives rise; it defines the moral tone of the reformer. We would have to be gods to meet such Herculean tasks, and Royce knows that the work is infinite. That is why he avers that God completes what in our finitude we must leave undone, making the gradual perfection of the world the joint venture of the human and the divine.

The introduction of God is at once the recognition that the task is too great for us. Since the task is infinite, without God we face moral despair. But if God picks up the slack, we might as well leave him a little more to do and thereby make our lives a lot more comfortable. Caught between the demand to exhaust ourselves and the temptation to throw in the towel, we face the problem that however much we do, we know we accomplish much less than we should. The magnitude of our duties makes guilt a certainty, and such inevitable failure weakens moral resolve. William James, even though he believed in the importance of what he called "moral holidays," did not do much better. He thought that every conscious need imposes a demand on all the world, and in particular on anyone who can help, to meet it. Here again the resultant obligations are potentially infinite, with only finite resources to discharge them.

The contemporary version of certain moral failure and unavoidable guilt is James Rachels's view that there is no relevant moral difference between failing to aid people in a distant famine and killing them on the spot. If that is true, our duties never end; tithing to Oxfam still leaves us murderers. All the moral marvels for which we are responsible must, of course, be done in accordance with our own ideas of what is in the interest of distant and deeply different others. Our aid to them is wrapped in our values; in availing themselves of it, they see their desires, habits, and traditions beginning to change. Worse, we find ourselves rushing around in the futile attempt to intervene everywhere, attempting to fix what cannot be corrected, or what cannot be corrected by us, or what we have no business trying to correct. The frustration and mischief that arise can be eliminated only if we embrace our finitude, respect the integrity of others, and allow people to conduct their lives as they see fit.

Letting others pursue their goods according to their own lights is a vital condition of autonomy. But even those who value self-determination or liberty tend to think of letting others be as a special duty imposed in certain circumstances rather than as a pervasive moral disposition. The better view is to conceive neutrality with regard to others as the foundational moral attitude of which obligations constitute a temporary suspension. The justification of this attitude and the grounding assumption of freedom is that human beings are self-moving agents who are capable of recognizing, seeking, and attaining their own good. If we deny human intelligence, drive, and competence, we will naturally wish to take over the lives of others to help them along. But this assessment of human ability is scurrilous and flies in the face of facts. If even dogs in heat know what is good for them and often attain it, there is little reason to suppose that humans don't and can't.

Of course, those who speak of the good tend to have high standards in mind, explaining to all why they should seek what, left alone, it would never occur to them to desire. However, this is but another case of imposing values on people who may well want to have no part of them. I do not wish to deny that under special circumstances others may know more about one's good than one knows oneself, but that is exceptional and rare. For the most part, being oneself day and night gives one a privileged view of what satisfies; there is little basis for substituting the judgments of others for our long experience and considered opinions. What appear to some as errors in valuation may in fact express the deep, authentic, and internally justified commitments of different others.

Establishing the disposition to let others be as a fundamental moral attitude is not capitulating to selfishness. Egoists typically maintain the dominance or the sole legitimacy of a single good. People who gladly leave others alone tend to do so, admittedly, to pursue their own projects. Their focus on their plans does not imply, however, that only their own projects are worth pursuing. On the contrary, the attitude makes sense solely on the assumption of the legitimacy of a plurality of goods. This multiplicity of values, each centered in a feeling agent, is what makes the need not to interfere in the lives of others compelling. For each life has a native judge and advocate; individuals are in the best position to determine their own interests and to devote energy to their own pursuits. People who let others work for their own good unimpeded simply do so out of their respect for the self-defining agency of which personhood consists. Claiming to know what is good for others and attempting to make them live up to it look much more like the work of selfishness than does keeping ourselves benignly at a distance. Distance from people may be motivated by indifference to them. I am perfectly happy to leave the lake alone, because it simply does not matter to me. I don't rush over to tend it when a speedboat slashes its face, and I don't grieve when it freezes in the winter. An attitude of this sort toward human beings, however, strikes me as horrendous; connected to one another from cradle to grave, we cannot be indifferent to one another's fates. The distance I advocate has its source not in cold unconcern, but in caring. Humans tend to do particularly well when they can make their own decisions and enjoy enough operational space to carry them out. If we wish others well, we let them flourish as they will, cheering them on from a distance. Good wrestlers and runners need no help from us; all we need to do is stay out of their way.

The flip side of leaving others alone because we want them to do well is helping them when the need arises. If we wish everyone well, we must be ready to aid them in emergencies or when obstacles are overwhelming. Wise people wait until the desire for help is obvious, if not through overt request, then through crushing circumstance or pleading eyes. To give true help is to become an instrument of the other's will, honoring the integrity of what the needy want instead of telling them what they ought to have. Moral wisdom consists largely in knowing when to leave people alone and when to help them and, when helping them, how not to subvert their aims.

In addition to being morally suspect, taking over other people's lives is also strategically unwise. The bears of Yellowstone Park got used to tourists bringing them food. As any intelligent creature would, they quickly abandoned foraging and took up favored spots near the highway, rendering themselves dependent on the kindness of people. We can find a trace of this tendency in human beings, some of whom raise no objections to being provided with what they need. Those wishing to interfere in the lives of others must therefore be ready to acquire permanent dependents who require continuing attention. Social welfare systems operate in disregard of this fact of human nature; instead of helping people over the hump, they offer ongoing support, tempting individuals to surrender responsibility for their own fates.

Helping others, therefore, is a far more complicated affair than it may at first appear. It must not be done in a way that impedes acknowledgment that people are intelligent choosers and independent agents. Paradoxically perhaps, providing for others may be of no help to them; it may invite them to surrender their independence and throw themselves on the mercy of strangers. The consequent inactivity, vulnerability, and collapse of self-respect interfere with even minimal satisfactions and make for a disconsolate life. The art of helping others begins with the recognition that giving does not always help. Just as courage does not mean tackling every danger, so caring does not demand that we answer every call.

But, it can be objected, is this not substituting our judgment for that of needy people, and if so, do we not wrongly interfere in their lives? The answer to both questions is no. Although refusing aid has important consequences for the people seeking it, it is primarily a decision about the activities of the donor. Such decisions are exercises in self-determination; in making them, we form an opinion only about how we ought to act and say nothing about what anybody else should do or aim to be. One's actions determine, first and foremost, one's own life. To leave others alone is simply to keep one's distance, and not a subtle way of exercising power over them.

Permitting others to seek their goods in their own ways tacitly acknowledges the existence of multiple perfections—that is, of many ways in which good lives may be led. Since all of these lives seem natural and appropriate to the people attracted to them, it becomes easy to recognize any claim of exclusive naturalness as a local illusion. Like each language, every life is natural when viewed from the inside, but alien to the unfriendly observer. The ubiquity of the natural destroys extravagant assertions of universal normativity. If natures differ, so must the values they seek and the experiences that satisfy them. We can match aims, values, and fulfillments to natures, but there is no independent standard in terms of which natures can be ranked.

Curbing our desire to rule over people and abandoning the error of supposing that ours is the only natural or worthy way to live would go a long distance toward making this a more decent world. There is an attitude to life that makes attainment of these difficult goals a little more likely, though it is itself not easy to sustain. The attitude I have in mind expresses the conviction that although some things matter intensely, most things don't matter much at all. In its current state of development, the human psyche is easily riled. Powerful emotions are released by relatively trivial events and observations: good looks engage our sexual machinery, and earrings worn by a male child can subvert peace within the family. Deviations from the customary evoke disproportionately violent responses, as when wearing the cap of the traditional rival of the local sports team leads to fights and when a casual joke or mild criticism plunges emotionally fragile people into deep despair.

We live as universal sensoria tuned to react to everything untoward in the world. We seem to have preferences about all things and get "bent out of shape" whenever things don't go our way. We seem never to ask the question "What is that to me?" and in good conscience to remind ourselves that a host of things are simply not our business. We like it better if we can feel outrage or at least anger, and minimally worry and concern, about the ways of the world. We don't like to admit that there is much we cannot change and that even if we could, it would make little difference to us except to please our prissy sense of order. Why should we want the world to line up the way we imagine it to be proper? The conceit that we know how people should behave, events work out, and the stars align themselves is laughable, yet we never seem to find it hilarious.

I want to be sure I am not misunderstood. There are plenty of things that should concern us in the most profound way. Suffering and joy matter, as does the humaneness of human relations. Undeserved ill, cruelty, injustice, and early death should engage our efforts. We must be ready to take a stand against activities that threaten to harm humans and other living creatures. But many of the things that most exercise our minds are nothing compared to such serious business. What religion others choose to practice, their private sex lives, their eating habits, their manner of speech, the way they click their tongues and roll their eyes, the veritable cornucopia of their peculiarities amount to less than is worthy of mention, never mind of outrage and retaliation. If someone chooses not to bathe, we have the option of distance; if people want group sex, we can decline to join the crowd. The joy of choice is that we can look the other way. Instead of trying to crush those of a different persuasion, we can affirm our own values by clinging to them tenaciously as the right ones for us.

We cannot calculate the harm that has come from the conviction that everything, or a large number of things, matter for our welfare and that therefore the world should operate just so. Yet how can it affect my good if others worship the wrong god or the right god in the wrong way? Is it really a disaster if my neighbors enjoy open marriages and members of some political parties closed minds? Does it make sense to fight over what to eat for dinner, where to put the couch, and whom never to invite again? These and many other issues have no significance, and in any case, whatever arrangement prevails soon passes away. But even nonexistence fails as a haven: some couples can't leave their history alone, rehearsing old hurts in the quest to wound again.

If anything doesn't matter, it is the past. A modest amount of reflection is adequate to learn what one can from old mistakes; for the rest, we need to liberate ourselves from concern over the unchangeable. Yet we find it difficult to forgive even those we love, new wars are started to settle old scores, and people who were never masters are invited to pay those who were never slaves huge sums in reparation for what happened to individuals long dead. The impulse to view everything as significant and hence demanding rectification will not let go of our minds, converting us into restless souls grotesquely busy with the attempt to reform, adjust, and regulate the world. The result is frustration and pain, without much headway in making anything better.

The commitment to leave others alone and the conviction that many things in life do not matter are connected, but they are not the same. We may decide to get out of the way of other people even though we think that what they do is both significant and annoying. Conversely, we may believe that many things don't matter, yet invade the autonomy of others out of wickedness or as nihilistic entertainment. Nevertheless, the commitment and the conviction go naturally together, each reinforcing the other in the quest for a sensible life. Thinking that only a relatively few things should be allowed to disturb our equilibrium invites us to let others explore their own concerns. In turn, the more we see others busying themselves with their own lives, the less we are tempted to believe that what they do is of significance to us. The result is improvement in the moral tone of society and a corresponding increase in human happiness.

My discussion of what cuts against appreciation of the different can serve as an outline of the obstacles in the way of a generous pluralism. Is fostering a variety of values, styles of life, and types of person worth the price? I have already indicated that leaving others alone and believing that lots of things that happen hold little significance for us would yield important benefits. But many people love the comfort of belonging and the exhilaration of persecuting the different much more than they delight in sympathy for the alien or a just distribution of happiness. Therefore, it may well be that people in tightly knit, intolerant communities live more satisfying lives than those who have to deal with the disquieting challenges and demanding sensitivities of strangely different people in their midst.

That this is not a far-fetched conjecture is amply displayed by the internal concord of Spartan society and by the unproblematic calm of religious communities and of medieval Japan. Such little worlds can have their own problems and crises, but they are not typically due to the disintegration of their value consensus. What attracts people to them is that the rightness of their customs receives reinforcement from all sides; no one defies the prevailing powers or denies the truth of shared ideas. Revealingly, we think of such agreement as a hallmark of heaven, where we enjoy praising the Lord in unison. Isolated fishing villages share this unanimity with the afterlife; in spite of their poverty, they provide a satisfactory social life due to concord about everything that matters.

Such uniformity of opinion and action is not a matter of choice for us, and it is quickly becoming unavailable for other communities as well. The mobility of people, the easy accessibility of vast stores of information, and the secularization of the world make it impossible for any nation to be a closed religious community or a modern Sparta. In some places, dissent and deviance are crushed and a coerced conformity appears to prevail for a while. But before long, imposed customs begin to crack and individual choice reestablishes alternative values and discordant modes of life. Despite efforts to control immigration, much of the world is now America, mixing races, religions, and ethnicities in ways that both break down and enrich original cultures. In the United States the pluralism of values, religions, lifestyles, characters, customs, and preferences is a fact to be dealt with, not a choice to be made. It makes no sense to ask if we should opt for a homogeneous or a widely diversified society; pluralism is simply unavoidable.

This suggests that wisdom lies in tolerating the pluralism we find, permitting African Americans, Hispanics, gays, people of underappreciated ethnicity, transsexuals, and pacifists to carve out what existence they can in a society that is no longer overtly antagonistic toward them. The principle of leaving others alone recommends this passive attitude to what others do; accepting them and letting them do what they wish is tantamount to welcoming them into the community. Anyone who knows the history of exclusion will think this not a small matter. Historically, minorities by choice or nature have faced insuperable obstacles to full participation in the benefits of social life. They have been denied schooling, the vote, the right to hold property, the choice of occupation and of marriage partners, free movement, medical care, and sometimes even existence itself. The moral improvement of the human race has rendered these cruelties exceptional and unacceptable events. They still occur here and there, but the weight of public opinion and the might of civilized nations militate against them. A passive pluralism, tolerating a wide variety of values and allowing people of all sorts full social participation should be enough to fulfill the requirements of moral decency.

What duty demands, however, is inadequate for flourishing. Even the apple people sought to diversify the one fruit that fell to their lot, and they did so with good reason. Comforting as uniformity may be, in the end it does not satisfy. Boredom with the same is an attractive alternative to insecurity in times of stress, but when things settle down, we start searching for the excitement that only the different can provide. This desire for variety may be inscribed in the curious, that is exploratory, nature of humans and animals. But even if it is not, we find it everywhere, suggesting that its satisfaction is a vital element of the fulfillment we seek. And indeed there is ample evidence that people who enjoy a combination of stability and change are more satisfied than those who enjoy either one without the other.

For this reason and for others, therefore, pluralistic society is, on the whole and within limits, more conducive to human flourishing than one that is uniform and inbred. I say "on the whole" because living in the midst of competing values is not an unmixed blessing; for people of rigid habits and firm convictions, putting up with what they may well think is wrong can entail distress. Only on balance, after factoring in the pain, is it appropriate to judge pluralistic societies to be better. And I say "within limits" because diversity can be so great, although that is certainly not a problem in our country today, that it destroys the shared values on which a society is based.

The positive pluralism to which this points requires not just the toleration of diversity but also its encouragement. Different cuisines, divergent ways of relating to family, a variety of religious practices, and multiple conceptions of self and occupation serve as John Stuart Mill's "experiments in living," without which many of the best approaches to dealing with our problems may well go unexplored. There is much to learn from the accumulated experience of other cultures and divergent traditions, and there is a special lesson in seeing that ethnic groups that in their original homes were mortal enemies can peacefully coexist in a country that values them all. Variety provides us with choice, and choice comes with the opportunity to develop ourselves in directions we could not have imagined on our own.

The pains attendant on positive pluralism are easier to bear if we keep in mind the principle that many things in life don't matter much. Gay marriage, for example, evokes visceral responses from many people. This may be a battle over words, in which case it could perhaps be resolved by calling legally sanctioned gay lifetime commitments "unions" instead of "marriages." But to the extent it is not, we could sensibly ask ourselves what it is about single-sex relationships that matters so much that we are prepared to throw generosity to the wind and deny gay people the protections of the laws. How does it affect me if two men in Seattle or two women on a Florida beach pledge to each other their eternal love? I realize that deeply felt religious beliefs play an important role in the refusal to permit such things. But does it weaken one's religious resolve if others don't agree with it and if worldly authorities don't enforce its edicts? Conversion is of value only if voluntary; conformity achieved by bayonets cannot please a decent deity.

The same holds for many of the other fierce battles in the so-called culture wars. The bitterness and intensity of the conflicts reveal that they are struggles for power—that is, attempts to make others do what we want. Very little in the way of substantive human welfare lies at the bottom of these controversies: no one's life or happiness hangs on whether we may display the Ten Commandments in a courthouse or outrageous paintings in a museum. For the most part, the source of the trouble is bruised sensitivities. People take offense at seeing what they don't like in public spaces and launch campaigns to stifle harmless expressions of opinion. One of the heartening moral developments of the past fifty years is growing sensitivity to the sensitivities of others. Unfortunately, however, sensitivities seem to expand in direct proportion to the willingness of people to respect them. If we recognized the readiness to act hurt as an instrument of controlling others, a calmer moral tone might begin to suffuse our public conversations.

Positive pluralism opens us to the joy of diversity. Once we overcome our dread of the different, the richness of the world engulfs us as a wave and leaves our cleansed souls with gratitude and amazement. We become like the apple people when they stumble upon a garden of bananas, strawberries, and grapes and realize for the first time all that they had missed. With them as with us, variety gives life; the multiplicity of values serves as food to build strong selves. We could never be the individuals we are if other people were not delightfully, resolutely, and in some cases radically different.

2

OPERATIONAL INDEPENDENCE

HUMAN LIFE USED to be cheap. In many parts of the world it still is. People were, and in some places still are, slaughtered without a second thought. They were expected to fight to the death in wars, die without complaint in famines, and perish for lack of medical attention. Women were raped and killed, prisoners were tortured, and children were enslaved. Tamerlane built pyramids out of human skulls; other conquerors competed for the honor of having butchered the largest number of people. Death could come swiftly and for trivial reasons to anyone weak or not born into the nobility.

By contrast with this, people in civilized countries have reached an advanced stage in the development of sensitivity. They sympathize with the plight of others and believe that human life represents a preeminent value. They have established institutions to protect the right of each person to exist and want to honor the claim of people on whatever resources a decent life requires. They punish murder and mayhem under a criminal code they try to apply impartially, and they refuse to countenance arbitrary persecutions and executions. For these people, life is longer and immeasurably better, because they care for others and live in friendly cooperation with them.

Caring for others, however, can go too far. It can lead to taking over the lives of other people by making choices that are theirs to make and relieving them of responsibility for what they do. In the name of kindness, it can also render people inactive by making it unnecessary for them to engage the world in pursuit of the things we need to live. Our protective love of children carries us in this direction. Government programs to take care of the disadvantaged and the unemployed can also turn into invitations to surrender a life of agency and become satisfied with what others do for us.

This raises the question of what we owe others. The Bible admonishes us never to harden our hearts, but it doesn't say enough about how far we have to go in softening them. In many circumstances only a morally insensitive or blatantly wicked person would turn away from helping those in need. But in many others, help may not be necessary or may even lead to long-term harm. The cruel past of humankind and our sympathy with all who suffer incline us to want to help everywhere. We think it a moral outrage for some to flourish while others have to make do with little, so we set out to even the scales and correct nature. Doing so, however, is a dangerous enterprise: our intentions tend to be good, but the consequences of our interventions are difficult to foresee.

Focusing on what we must do for our fellows, moreover, presents only a partial and therefore misleading picture of our moral relations to them. We must also ask when it is all right to invade the lives of other people. Under what circumstances are we justified in *not* leaving others alone? One may think it absurd, of course, to consider it an invasion of people's independence if we save them from dying of hunger. But even there, conditions may obtain that make such an act morally suspect, as when the person we want to save chooses to be on a hunger strike. Further, the bulk of our interactions involve nothing as dramatic as this. Everyday incursions take the form of telling people what they should eat, instructing them on how to raise their children, and demanding justifications for their actions. This sort of meddling is a favorite and deeply satisfying activity of many people, some of whom cannot understand why others, strangers no less than friends, fail to avail themselves of their wisdom.

Decent people concern themselves with human flourishing, as helping others is a fundamental moral task. But the world would be a horrible place if people spent their time telling each other what to do and making them do it. For such activities take away from others what is properly theirs: decisions about how to run their lives.

Collaboration leads to the ever growing dependence of humans on one another. Much of what we accomplish presupposes the skills and achievements of previous generations and the work of innumerable contemporaries. Medical knowledge, for example, builds up over centuries; adding to it requires tens of thousands of researchers and treatment professionals. Improvements in transportation and communication require institutions that organize the activities of many individuals and whose existence spans generations.

This makes it look as if all skills and activities were, in the end, social possessions. The impression is supported by the centrality of education in human life. Our meager physical endowment—we come into the world without even fur or scales—is matched by how little we can do at birth. Parents know that it takes a long time to arm children with the most rudimentary skills; two decades of the efforts of teachers barely suffice to acquaint the young with a portion of the accumulated wisdom of the human race. This vast store of knowledge, acquired over thousands of years of experience, is the property of no single mind. It exists in books; in communally conceived and executed products, such as bridges; and in the intelligent practices of cooperating human beings. From this perspective, individuals appear to be created by social processes to which they add little and which they cannot control.

Much as we find this picture beguiling, it presents only the obvious half of the truth. In our busy communal lives we tend to overlook the deeper reality that all activity is the work of individuals. Society is not an agent in the physical world; flesh-and-blood persons are. Institutions cannot continue to exist without the compliant labor of the people who constitute them, and every one of the many acts necessary to summon airplanes and dams into existence is performed by some single person voluntarily. Everything hangs on what people do: a corporation would disintegrate if its employees decided not to defend its interests. The entire social world is pieced together out of the contributions of individuals and unravels when they decide to stop.

That everything depends on the actions of living persons is amply demonstrated by general strikes, which can paralyze society. Work slowdowns and employees calling in sick remind us of the same point: human practices continue only because people fall in line and show themselves willing to continue them. We express this truth about the locus of agency when we say that one can take a horse to water but cannot make it drink, and we experience it when we try, unsuccessfully, to make teenagers do what we think they should. A bank whose tellers paid scant attention to their cash, whose managers did not care about who failed to come to work, whose auditors shrugged their shoulders at signs of embezzlement, and whose board of directors met only to party would soon go out of business. It would cease to be a functioning organization, because the organisms that made it work lost interest in promoting its interests. Agency resides in organisms, not in organizations.

People living in a world of large institutions, however, find it advantageous to deny that they have the power to destroy apparently omnipotent organizations. The ability to stop it all imposes great responsibilities, and when institutions operate in a way that is inhumane or morally corrupt, individuals must refuse to cooperate. Since this demands great courage and can lead to grievous consequences, people often decide to go along with whatever is demanded of them, hiding behind the excuse that one person cannot accomplish much by resisting.

In reality, however, the action of the organization is but the sum of the actions of its members, and there are times when a bold moral challenge issued by a single individual is enough to bring the entire house of cards to the ground. This phenomenon is what Václav Havel referred to as "the power of the powerless," employing that paradoxical phrase to call attention to the might of the "little" person. There is nothing paradoxical about this power, however, unless we begin with the false assumption that anything other than individuals can act. The established power of institutions can, of course, cause the individual to be swept away, but that is the inherent danger of moral action and the mark of an uncivilized society.

If Gandhi had resisted the Nazis, he would have been shot at once; the relatively civilized British could not find an adequate excuse or reason to remove him. The crude display of military might at Tiananmen Square was possible only because soldiers acted like machines and did not refuse to massacre their fellow citizens. This is in sharp contrast to the peaceful transformation of the Ukraine in 2005 and other silent revolutions in which no one dared give the order to fire, or when they did, no one followed it. So the greatest danger to the moral agent is a morally insensitive society; individuals always have the power to cry halt, but their best chance of success is when their fellows realize that they, too, can resist.

Some thinkers suppose that institutions and states are purposive beings that formulate plans and take steps to enact them. People in decision-making positions can, of course, identify ends for the organization or collection of people they lead, but these are plans for the group rather than of it as a unified agency. Single-purpose institutions such as restaurants come closest to the concentrated action typical of individuals, but their focused exertions fall far short of the effortless integration of personal acts. Larger collections of people such as cities and states display contrary currents of opinion and action; if individuals showed the aimlessness and indecision of communities, we would have to give them the protections due children and the mentally ill.

Some visionaries fancy that the relation of individuals to their communities or nations is precisely analogous to the relation of cells to the organisms of which they are parts. They reason that both cells and persons serve a larger whole and find life and significance only in that service. In their view the integration of the body is matched by the order of the state, and in both cases this reveals a hierarchy of importance: cells and individuals are equally dispensable, but while they live, they must serve their lord and master.

We know organisms that, observed from a distance, seem to relate to their social context in this way. Ants, for example, appear to enact a narrative of individual insignificance, and bees show no reluctance to die for their hive. Possibly some future humans also will live in thrall of their community, surrendering themselves to the service of the larger whole. But that is clearly not how things stand now. Admittedly, people are capable of stunning acts of self-sacrifice in protecting others. But sacrifice is not surrender; it flows from private decision and is the act of a self-possessed, independent agent.

This is not to deny the influence of the social milieu on the individual. What others do is noted by children and often adopted as their mode of operation. The values of the crowd are contagious, and many people find it nearly impossible to live according to private principles or to enact unconventional patterns of life. The culture in which we live stamps us with its marks to such an extent that we become easily identifiable as, say, twenty-first-century Americans or Egyptians from the age of Cleopatra. But social influence flows from person to person, and the actions it incites are performed by individual agents. There are no magical social causes other than what individuals singly or conjointly do.

The ultimate reason for the primacy of personal action is biological; its fruit is moral. The human race is fragmented into individuals, each of whom is an agent entrusted with taking care of itself and endowed by nature with the tools to do so. Normally we can find food, defend ourselves, chart a course of life, and find mates to reproduce the species. Although there is much we cannot do without the cooperation of our fellows, the cooperation itself presupposes that we are self-moving organisms capable of contributing to what others do. We must be able to work our parts, frame purposes, and respond to circumstance or else be no better than logs on the forest floor. Humans, like cats, are ornery: only they can operate their bodies, and they do largely what they want.

Autonomous agency, then, is founded on the biological reality that organisms are self-governing centers of energy. They are not boulders in a meadow, inert and without transformative insides, but dynamic and often unpredictable wellsprings of activity. The outside world can affect them, but it gets back something different from what it offered. Just as the bee turns pollen into honey and our bodies convert fried chicken into blood and tissue, so living souls build external influences into their substance. Although they are not detached from the world in origin and sustenance, they nevertheless operate as independent agents.

One can imagine circumstances, albeit not particularly interesting ones, in which agency is not nodular. In such a world energy flows as in a field from one relatively undifferentiated portion of space to another. Individuation is incomplete, with fluid and permeable boundaries between beings. Charles Sanders Peirce conceived the relation of minds on this model, with the ideas of which they consist spreading in all directions, mixing and interpenetrating in the process. This may be a good description of how ideas behave in the public domain, where they are shared through books, social media, and conversations. But that is not how fully individuated biological organisms operate. They are self-directing bundles of energy, actively engaged in maintaining their integrity and developing themselves according to plan or native pattern.

Both self-preservation and self-development point to a purposiveness in the service of which the organism deploys its energies. The teleology is present in plants but becomes particularly notable in animals, whose exertions are directed largely at accomplishing what they want. The level of self-possession or self-control this requires marks the organism as a self-contained agent capable of operating without external help: it plans, executes, and assesses its own activities. Its independence is central for understanding its nature; it moves of its own accord, even if—or perhaps especially when—it is left to its own devices. Under normal circumstances it needs little help to do what it wants and insists, as children do, on being left alone to pursue its purposes.

Reliance on the external environment for food and air in the case of the organism and for language and the skills of culture in the case of socialized humans takes nothing away from this independence. The things we need in order to operate amount to background conditions of life that neither act through us nor determine what we do. The enabling conditions of action do not themselves act; only organisms do. And when they do, the immediate source of their operation and its ultimate controlling force are they themselves.

This independence is on display in much of what human beings do. What we call "pigheadedness" in pursuit of a goal, dogged rejection of external interference, and the well-known but maddening insistence of people on deciding how to do things and when are manifestations of the desire to be in charge of one's life. We see the demand for self-governance even in children as they try, at an early stage of existence, to wrest decision-making power from their parents. Adults retain the tendency to display it in their resentful resistance to orders from above. Even sick and old people are devoted to self-determination, attempting to control the time and manner of their demise.

Individuals, like spinning tops, live their lives with a momentum all their own. As existentialists insist, they make their decisions and bear the consequences alone. No matter how much social support they receive, in the end they enjoy their pleasures, suffer as a result of their mistakes, and face their deaths in ultimate isolation. This does not mean that their minds are impenetrable to others or that the community abandons them in their hours of need. But no one is able to lift the burden of failure from another, and no one can share the infinite grief of seeing a beloved partner leave the world. There is a vast difference between knowing what others suffer and suffering those things oneself; the issue is not the knowability of other minds, but the utter existential insularity of each.

All of this points to an important but often overlooked distinction. Ontologically—that is, from the perspective of their existence—people are clearly dependent. They cannot come into existence without parents; they rely on air, food, and water for life; and they would be worse off than wild animals if others had not cared for them, taught them, and continued to provide them with many of the necessities of life. Operationally, on the other hand, individuals are largely independent. They are able to move and control their parts and to coordinate them in order to engage in the activities with which they busy themselves day and night. They frame purposes and execute them, focusing their efforts on attaining what they want. They do this without help from others and reach a level of satisfaction they deem adequate, if only for the moment.

Ontological or ultimate dependence takes nothing away from the operational independence of organisms. Automobiles cannot function without motor and gas, yet the necessary conditions of such operation determine neither what they do nor where they go. So it is with organisms, except that humans and other animals do not wait to have their tanks filled and their motors fixed; they take action to feed themselves and to repair the damage to their bodies. Under normal circumstances they are in need of little or nothing beyond their own power in order to operate; they are planning, self-structuring, self-motivating, self-moving, and self-satisfying beings. Even quadriplegics enjoy a residue of this complex and marvelous ability in speaking, eating, and regulating the parts of their bodies whose movement is not denied them.

People who insist on the communal nature of all activity announce it on their own, without aid. Thinkers who maintain that since language is a social product, their ideas are not really their own, think this alone, in the quiet of their studies. Others, who are able to see only social action and no individual initiative, write their own books and get paid for lecturing about them. The operational independence of humans and animals surrounds us on all sides; the fragmentation of the life force into individuals renders it an unavoidable reality. The refusal to see it must be due to an overwrought sense of solidarity with others or to an unrealistically low opinion of one's own agency.

Every denial of individual agency or operational independence is its affirmation; the action might serve some imagined social good, but it is executed by an individual person. Why anyone would be tempted to suppose otherwise sheds light on the radical changes human life has undergone in the last few thousand years. Primitive hunters pursuing their prey, mothers in a cave giving birth, and solitary warriors struggling to survive would never have supposed that their actions were anything but their own. They could rely only on themselves; at any rate, no one could or would help them much, and instinct or experience enabled them to make it through another day. Some measure of cooperation was present even then, of course; it took two to beget children, and someone had to cook the beast the hunter killed. But the coordination of activities was minimal, rarely going beyond volunteering or acquiescing in some act in return for another.

Increase in the population, division of labor, and consequent growth of the scope and complexity of action have made humans vastly more interdependent. Our actions have become cooperative on a scale that would have been unimaginable to primitive peoples, and by means of these actions we have acquired significant control over some aspects of nature. The construction of airplanes and the operation of airlines, for example, require the precisely correlated labor of tens of thousands of people. Such activities confer immense power on us, although the power does not belong to any single person. The acts are not anyone's either; they are too large to be appropriated by individuals, each of whom makes but a minuscule contribution to them.

The natural supposition is that acts of this sort are intrinsically social, and some may even be tempted to think they are performed by some super-organism, such as American Airlines or the state of France. In fact, however, no such super-organisms exist; institutions and nations are simply interacting individuals coordinated in their voluntarily assumed tasks. The moment significant numbers of people refuse to do their jobs, the institution disintegrates like a soap bubble. Something like this happened in the Soviet Union before its disappearance. The acts themselves are social only in the sense that it takes many people to perform them and that some persons plan and control the activities of others. Control, however, must be understood in a soft sense, for planners cannot make their colleagues do what they want; they can only make it worth their while to engage in the desired behavior. This means that the causation involved runs through the choice mechanisms of workers, making them the ultimate agents performing the necessary acts.

The mistake of thinking that large-scale achievements are social originates in amazement at the scope and power of the actions of institutions and neglect to analyze them into their constituents, which are act fragments performed by individuals. The failure of analysis disguises the fact that speaking of institutional actions is just a shorthand way of referring to masses of individual activities. This simplification of speech obscures important moral realities, enabling people to believe that since questionable actions look as though they were performed by faceless institutions, they are relieved of responsibility. The sense of personal powerlessness is at once a defense against the charge of irresponsibility: if I did not cause or cannot change the status quo, I cannot be charged with having done less than decency demands.

American English is guilty of this problematic simplification; for the most part, the English spoken in Britain is not. There, words such as "Microsoft," although they appear to be the names of single entities, nevertheless function as collective nouns, referring to the multiplicity of the people constituting the company. Accordingly, in tacit acknowledgment of the ontology of action, they take plural verbs, suggesting that institutions masquerading as unified agents are in fact associated collections of activities. So, for example, "Microsoft hires 100 new employees" is an incorrect and misleading way of speaking; in Britain the proper way of reporting such facts takes the form of "Microsoft hire 100 new employees," because hiring is a complex set of activities by a large number of people instead of a single act by an institution.

Highly coordinated acts of momentous complexity and scope are common in the commercial world in this age of large institutions and populous nation-states. Connecting hundreds of cities by means of air service appears to be the effortless achievement of huge corporations. In reality, however, the act is neither single nor effortless; it consists of innumerable act fragments contributed by tens of thousands of people. Some decide which cities to serve and at what hours of the day; others fuel the planes and load the baggage; the pilots take responsibility for flying passengers safely from one place to another; ticket vendors sell seats; gate agents make sure that only ticketed passengers board; mechanics service the planes; accountants keep the books of the company and pay its employees; and thousands of other people in hundreds of other specialist assignments take pains to ensure that everything runs smoothly.

Institutions consist of such chains of mediation, in which each participant acts on behalf of others or in concert with them. The impression of the rational agency of corporations is greatly bolstered by the experience of people working for them: the acts to which the employees contribute are so vast that they literally do not know them. Situated in the bowels of an institution, they have little understanding of the total act to which they contribute and no sense of control over it. Although they are busy doing a hundred things, they feel passive and powerless to change their routines. They suspect that the acts in which they participate may have harmful consequences, but they deflect responsibility for them by reference to the impotence they feel. They know that their fellow workers are in a position no different from theirs, so they cannot be blamed either. It must, therefore, be the institution, "the system," that is at fault.

This line of reasoning creates the mistaken impression that institutions are agents. Living human beings make the plans of institutions, and others execute the plans, even if each participant contributes only a little. There is no need to postulate any agency beyond what all of these individuals do. The act of the institution is fully analyzable into the constituent actions of human beings; if there is credit or blame, it rests squarely on the shoulders of people, not on some super-entity whose actions encompass us. Although it is understandable that people in mediated chains should see themselves as passive and the system in which they operate as active, this inverted perspective has the undesirable effect of allowing them to think they have no moral responsibility for the actions they perform on behalf of their nations or their employers. The past century saw this denial of responsibility among Nazi and Soviet concentration camp guards and in the silent complicity of employees in the white-collar business crimes of their bosses.

It may be objected, however, that the analysis of institutional acts into the actions of individuals doesn't go far enough. Just as social acts are made up of what people do, so the actions of individuals may be reduced to the movements of the cells of their bodies. In fact, as indicated earlier, some people think they can establish the insignificance of individuals by means of the analogy between the relation of cells to the bodies they constitute and the relation of individuals to institutions, communities, or nations. Cells are created to serve the larger whole, and any one or set of them is dispensable and easily replaced. Similarly, individuals are supposed to be products of the social whole, and hence their fulfillment is inseparable from the self-sacrificing service they provide. Why should we stop the analysis at individual action and not proceed to the work of cells or body parts?

This way of posing the question of the proper range of analysis is helpful and revealing. How far we analyze and what categories we use are matters of decision, and such decisions are made for reasons, all of which relate to human flourishing. Humans can do a world of harm to each other, to other living creatures, and to the planet on which they live. Without a system of holding people accountable for what they do, the harm would be potentially limitless.

The practice of imputing responsibility for actions is possible only if we take the agents to be individual persons. Could we punish corporations for misdeeds? The usual means of punishment are jail terms, fines, and execution. But the company cannot be put in prison, so we incarcerate its executives. Fining a corporation causes misery only to those it employs and to its shareholders. Its board of directors (consisting of individual agents) may learn a lesson, but the firm itself cannot be embarrassed or suffer pain. We can put the institution out of business, as the U.S. government did Arthur Andersen, but since companies are indifferent to life and death, such actions do not have the deterrent effect of an execution; the only ones who suffer and who could be expected to modify their behavior are its human employees. If we want to retain a system of moral responsibility, we must reject the thought that organizations or states are the ultimate agents in the world.

Similarly, we must not look below the level of individuals if the practice of holding agents accountable is to remain viable. If we did, the experienced operational independence of persons would disappear in their total reliance on the movements of parts of their bodies. With operational independence would go moral responsibility for one's acts; cells cannot be jailed, it makes no sense to cut off the arm that stabbed the victim in punishment for its misbehavior, and it would be absurd to blame one's ductless glands for battery or fraud. Even without going so far as to analyze the action of cells into the movement of molecules and those into the swirl of subatomic particles, we lose the human world we know if we take our eyes off the agency of people.

This is a perfectly good pragmatic argument for focusing on the actions of individuals and declaring persons to be the authors of whatever is done. Those who are not satisfied with pragmatic arguments might come to the same conclusion by reflecting on what an action is. Events or happenings clearly do not qualify; actions require reference to what the agent means to do. Intentions or purposes are, therefore, essential elements of actions, as are consequences, proposed and actual. Thus, an action is a complex and temporally extended unity of intention, execution, and result. We cannot know what an act is by looking at the plan or at the isolated doing; we learn what we have done only by seeing how the intention, as put into effect, plays in the real world.

Freedom involves the relation between intention and performance; it consists of the ability to frame purposes and to execute them. To enjoy liberty, the nineteenth-century British thinker John Stuart Mill pointed out, is to be able to do what we want—that is, to be unimpeded in planning for ourselves and to have the power to convert these plans into reality. The relation of what we do to its consequences, on the other hand, defines responsibility. So both freedom and responsibility are tied in with the notion of action. The idea is that as free we do what we want, and as responsible we bear the consequences. Properly understood, freedom and responsibility are two sides of the same coin and constitute indispensable conditions of education: we learn to adjust and limit our freedom on the basis of the outcomes of previous acts.

This notion of action finds no application to body parts, cells, proteins, and subatomic particles. None of these is in a position to frame purposes and to consider, let alone learn much from, consequences. Things happen that involve them, but they are not self-moving organisms that plan, execute their intentions, and enjoy or suffer the results. The same is true of institutions, organizations, states, and nations: they have no minds independent of the intelligence of their leaders, no muscles apart from the people who act under their banners, and no feeling to enjoy or suffer what they have created. Some higher animals may be able to undertake actions of the sort here described, but beyond them and angels—if it turns out that any such exist—only living human beings can act, and they always do so in their individual capacity.

3

LEAVING OTHERS ALONE

IF HUMANS ARE self-moving organisms that act and organize their lives on their own, the way to respect them is to leave them alone. Letting them be is to allow them to operate as they see fit, setting their own goals and working to reach them by their own efforts. This is appropriate for operationally independent organisms because, sensing their independence, they insist on framing their own purposes and charting their own course. We see this drive for self-determination even in young children and animals in their rejection of external influence over their behavior. We are like cats, turning our backs when others tell us what to do or clinging "pigheadedly" to our own ideas.

Respect for others consists primarily in acknowledging them as worthy decision makers or, as it is sometimes put, as autonomous or self-determining agents. On the positive side, this means that we accept them as authorities legitimately ruling over their own domain. Negatively, it is the commitment not to interfere in the affairs of other operationally independent agents, no matter how wrongheaded their decisions may seem to us. Seeing people as perpetually in need of intervention by others indicates not respect for them, but pity, for it implies that they are unable to take care of themselves. Handling their own affairs, by contrast, confers dignity on people and enables us to view them as no worse and no worse off than we are.

Babies are fed and clothed because they cannot take care of themselves. Much of growing up consists of acquiring operational skills. Little by little, children learn to eat and walk on their own, to choose their clothes and put on their shoes, to signal their intentions and to be safe in crossing the street. Good parents rejoice in this development: their love gains fulfillment in the independence of their offspring. Remaining a perpetual child requiring service and direction is a source of grief whose intensity is proportional to the need. Paradoxically perhaps, the aim of help is to make help unnecessary, which reveals that our idea of the normal state of individuals is independence of the ministrations of others.

Yet leaving others alone is a rare virtue and seems to go against some of our deepest tendencies. One might suppose that getting involved in other people's business is an expression of concern or of our social nature. In fact, however, we can be fully social and fulfill our responsibilities to others without taking over their lives. One can adopt the attitude of letting one's neighbors operate unimpeded so long as they allow us to do likewise. We can cheer them on and grieve with them, we can even help them when they ask or their situation demands it, but it is best to leave it to them to form their own values and plans.

A community of such self-determining yet caring individuals is conceivable and would be as close as humankind can get to peaceful perfection. As everything perfect, of course, it is unlikely to come about. Willfulness and egoism stand in its way and will not soon relinquish their hold on human nature. The egoism makes us believe that we know what is good for others better than they know it themselves. Our wills rejoice in subjecting the wills of others to our rule; nothing conveys our power more clearly than other people listening to us and doing our bidding. The result is a constant series of incursions into the lives of other people, with hardly a thought of how annoying *we* would find such interference.

Intervention is appropriate in the operation of young children so long as the primary purpose of it is their safety and gentle education. Mill significantly overstated this point when he said that the principle of liberty does not apply to children or to "young persons below the age which the law may fix as that of manhood or womanhood." Ignorance of how the world works may well get children in trouble, and on occasion they have to be protected from self-wrought harm. But even with them it is best to limit intervention to a minimum. Children who are not brought up to make choices tend to grow into adults who are indecisive in their actions and unsure of what they believe. Even the very young prize the independence of choosing their own clothes and food and deciding what they will do, how, and when. This may be inconvenient or annoying to adults, but nothing builds self-confidence and responsibility for one's actions more effectively than being permitted to act freely and experience the consequences.

Even when the consequences are foreseeably harmful, education may proceed with minimal intervention. Children who, fascinated by the red glow on top of the electric stove, want to touch it may be persuaded to put their hands on the heating element when it is still cold. Upon being turned on, the element heats gradually, giving young experimenters adequate time to withdraw their hands intact. The point is to view the activities even of children as self-motivated inquiries into the ways of the world and to guide their choices instead of crushing their initiatives.

Just as we find it difficult not to run the lives of our children, we feel sorely tempted to correct the mistakes of others. "Mistakes" tend to be defined as deviations from how *we* would do things, which in turn is equated with the natural or proper way to operate. We can offer multiple justifications for intervention: the purposes, values, or behavior of others may be declared unnatural, dangerous, or the result of cognitive malfunction. It seems to escape us that these justifications constitute weapons of intolerance that can be quickly deployed if our neighbors remain unrepentant. The ultimate argument on behalf of incursion is that it is done for the good of people who are viewed as having lost their way. In appearance, all such intervention is benign: telling others what to do or correcting their mistakes is displayed as a matter of caring whose aim is promotion of their good. Astonishingly, many who regularly wish to make decisions for others innocently believe their self-justifications and find it outrageous when their interference is rebuffed.

What accounts for this illusion of innocence? Many people mean well, and even more think that they do. The impression of benevolence is reinforced when we question our motives for intervention. We are quick to note that people doing what we desire offers us, for the most part, no material gain. Without the promise of substantial benefit to us, it is easy to suppose that our demand for compliance cannot be selfish. We simply do what we can to help lost souls find their way.

The illusion is reinforced by the conviction that our way of doing things is right. The source of our habits is of little moment; whether they derive from what we were taught or from values we constructed for ourselves, our practice confers conviction. Familiarity with what we do and success measured by its results make it virtually impossible to entertain alternative possibilities; it simply does not occur to us that what works well for one person may be intolerable for another.

Further, the contingency and changeability of one's habits tend not to be noticed. It should not be surprising, therefore, that we can innocently invite others to imitate what we do, for what we do now appears to be what we have always done. And when it comes to there being no tangible benefit to the imitation, what we forget is that the benefit is the imitation itself: success of one's will provides a greater joy than does physical gain. Material goods count as nothing compared to the prosperous exercise of the will.

A part of the reason for this is that physical well-being delights only if and because we want it. A number of thinkers have pointed out that pleasure amounts to successful operation of the will and pain consists of its frustration. What we want is so closely connected with the machinery of feeling and action in the human body that its fulfillment colors all of our emotional life. It may sound like a commonplace that we are creatures of desire and need, but it does so only because many of our days are spent in service to our will. To see the world take shape in response to our wishes is delight; to see human beings do things as a result of our influence exhilarates beyond the capacity to express it.

Thoughtful people can catch themselves attempting to impose their will upon virtually anything that gets in their way. Coat hangers hooked to one another and resisting order elicit fury. Dogs are ordered about to suit our idea of what they should do or where they should be. Children are told to do what is right, that is, what we want them to do, on pain of swift and painful consequences. Strangers in the supermarket take an interest in what we buy and propose behaviors they favor over our own. Older people tell us what to do, invoking their wide experience, while their children claim superior knowledge in the name of acquaintance with "the way things are now." If we look carefully, human reality reveals itself as a clash of wills, with everyone jockeying for position and attempting to prevail.

Those who equate devotion to our will with calculated selfishness are at a distance from the truth. In enacting our will, our intentions may be honorable and focus on what would be good for the people who surround us. On occasion, it may even be true that what we suggest is in fact better than what others propose to do. That, however, is rarely the real issue. At the center of the conflicts that ensue is not the question of whose will has greater merit, but simply that what one wants to do feels familiar and right and what others plan for one is alien. Selfishness suggests an element of intelligent calculation. The clash of wills, by contrast, often bypasses, disregards, or discards all reason; it is a struggle for power that can destroy friendships, love relations, families, and even the antagonists themselves.

The clash of wills torments not only lovers and neighbors. Much of the history of humankind is a record of people and peoples trying to make others do what they don't want. Tribal chieftains and kings wanted to subjugate individuals in their communities, nations fought hard to force other nations to surrender their land and treasure, advocates of aggressive religions desired to convert the world to their convictions, and races imposed their yoke on other races. Rarely has anyone stopped to ask what business it is of theirs to interfere in the lives of others and what difference it makes in the end if others are left alone to lead their lives the way they choose. Even if the salvation of one's soul is at stake, it is difficult to believe that God would want involuntary converts. We may well have the obligation to acquaint others with what we deem right and good, but that duty cannot extend to forcing them into the service of the God we worship. If upon being told of opportunities for salvation they nevertheless persist in their folly, they and they alone will have to bear the consequences.

What is it to me if others place themselves beyond redemption? Of course I care, but it is dangerous to think that I and I alone have found the secret of the righteous life. If others don't capitulate to my truth, the sensible response is not to crush them, but to see if my presumed knowledge might not need revision. Clinging to what we believe true is not an act of intellect, but of will. Intelligent people are shaped by the resistance of others to their supposed truths; they are ready to entertain any sensible idea and refuse to maintain their own at all costs. The bitterness of much intellectual feuding reveals that what is at stake in them is not principle but power.

The power is that of making others do what we want. A favorite way of exercising it is getting other people to do what is of benefit to us. For example, I can pretend to be ill and thereby occasion the neighbors to bring me food. They would not have done so had I not pleaded incapacity, and the effort and the expenditure of money are not in any obvious way in their interest. Yet my supposed plight puts them in a position that requires urgent action. Something similar occurs whenever we ask for a favor or make empty threats to achieve our ends. This style of behavior is widespread and learned early in life; even young children know how to manipulate their parents by cries and lamentations.

A more pernicious control over others takes the form of subjugating their wills to ours. In this case no external benefit accrues to the stronger; the delight is in the victory. The very act of making others do what we want, even if it does us no further good, floods many with satisfaction. The pleasure becomes more perverse when we have no particular desire other than to negate what others want. The cruelty of contravening whatever other people crave is what Schopenhauer said constitutes the very essence of wickedness. Frustrated parents come to mind, disciplining their children for harmless play, along with bureaucrats who set obstacles in the way of whatever one needs from their institutions.

Some people know how to develop this nasty contrariness into an art. A person of my acquaintance begins every response with the word "No," even when what follows indicates agreement with what has just been said. Partners in some marriages greet each other's suggestions with automatic rejection. Siblings tend to negate one another's beliefs and articulate opposing demands. Businesses crash and burn because the partners show greater interest in defeating one another's ideas than in seeing the enterprise succeed. Shockingly often, people would rather have nothing if they can't have their way.

Those who are sensitive to what goes on around us see that incessant interference in the affairs of others is a favorite activity of human beings. Its source may be benign interest in what others do or want, but it soon balloons into the attempt in small or large ways to take over the lives of friends, neighbors, and even strangers. Once established as a habit, interference tends to become automatic rather than reflectively benevolent, until people can no longer distinguish what is their business from what they have no right and no reason to tackle. This is what makes leaving others alone a rare virtue.

It is a virtue because the habits it involves express and promote human flourishing. They betoken satisfaction with guiding one's life without the need to order others about or to convert them to one's chosen ways. There is something magnificent about control directed upon oneself, resulting in an independently operating, intelligent, responsible, and persevering agent. The self-motivating person who takes no commands from others and needs no others to command comes close to the best the human race has produced. In such an individual, habits of independence are coupled with deep respect for the independence of others. The tendency to leave others alone is rooted not in indifference to the fate of people, but in the conviction that under normal circumstances we can benefit them most by letting them pursue their own ends without interference.

This deference to what other people think, plan, and do tends to yield excellent results in human relations. To be sure, some people experience difficulty in choosing goals for their lives and in summoning the energy to achieve them. I have had students who joined the army because they did not want to have to decide when to get up in the morning and how to spend their days. Others are raised in a way that even in retirement they seek the guidance of older people. But these are exceptions. Normally, young children fight for their independence, and unimpeded choice is the shining ideal of teenage rebellion. Nations under the yoke of an alien force resist the intruders without regard to the benefits they confer, and there are few acts that evoke greater fury than telling others what they ought to do. Most people like making their own decisions, not necessarily because they are the best, but because they are their own.

There is little doubt that from time to time we make mistakes about what is good for us. An ideally well-informed psychologist might know more about what would satisfy us than we do. Other people, observing us dispassionately, might see something about our actions that we miss. Most of the time, however, we enjoy the fruits of private immediacy with ourselves: we know what we want and what we enjoy directly and therefore better than any casual observer. A true science of psychology, offering insights into the private souls of individuals, has not yet been developed and may never be. Attentive outsiders can on occasion stumble upon an insight, and the longer people live with us, the more they are able to discern our patterns. Yet the approach from the outside is forever inadequate and often leads to grievous misunderstandings of who we are.

We enjoy making our own decisions, because doing so creates the feeling that we are in control of our lives. And indeed, up to a point we are, because both the principles that govern our choices and the actions that flow from them are ours. The natural unity of human actions requires that intention, action, and enjoyment or suffering of the results be lodged in one person. So long as we can plan and motivate ourselves to act on our purposes, we feel whole and satisfied in a way that is denied to those who execute alien plans or see their intentions subverted at the hands of others. Creating projects and doing what is necessary to realize them constitute some of the great pleasures of humankind.

The arrogance of people who, hardly knowing us, feel qualified to tell us what would satisfy is the source of recurring annoyance. They may see their invasion as innocent and well-meaning and their recommendations as beneficial, perhaps even necessary. But they miss exercising the imagination, a vital organ of the moral life, that would show them how angry they would be if someone else took the liberty of telling them what to do. Their censure of people who do not take their advice itself provides a hint of how highly they value their opinions and how fervently they treasure their self-determination.

The moral imagination constitutes our best hope of civilizing the human race. There were early signs of it in primitive cave paintings and in Native American rituals of asking the forgiveness of buffalo for taking their lives. Its essence is the precious ability to see others as similar to ourselves—that is, as conscious beings who treasure their lives. To value life is at once to embrace and celebrate one's autonomy. The operational independence of organisms carries with it a centralized decision-making and control structure. This is what interference by others threatens and death terminates. It may be too much to say that violations of one's autonomy are minor forms of death, but clearly there is an analogy, as every event of meddling breaks off the intimate connection between decision and enactment, rendering people incapacitated or inactive.

Exercise of the moral imagination is not the same as what William James and others call expansion of the ego. The latter consists of learning to see all manner of things and persons as vital parts of oneself. Ego expansion combats the narrow selfishness of people by breaking down the confines of the self, which allows us to see ourselves as complex and inclusive. The result is that our loved ones and neighbors, our clothes, house, and surroundings become incorporated into the self and are no longer viewed as alien.

This is a hugely useful development for human relations, for it eliminates the sharp distinction between self and other. Incorporating the other in oneself, however, does nothing to safeguard its distinct integrity. The moral imagination, by contrast, retains the separation of self and other but sees their lives and predicaments as identical. Empathy helps us acquire respect for other people as both sufferers and agents. By means of it we can learn to appreciate the joys and sorrows of individuals who are viewed not as parts of us, but as similarly afflicted creatures. It can also help us honor people as independent decision makers who want to retain the power to run their lives.

Seeing people as both sufferers and self-motivated agents is important for the moral life, but the latter is preeminently significant for human freedom. The conviction that others are feeling subjects may make us cry with them; recognizing that they are independent wills confers respect on their designs and operations. There are times, of course, at which the two tendencies work at cross-purposes or come in conflict. We find it difficult, for example, not to intervene when people are bent on hurting themselves. In fact, there is enough social agreement on this that self-destructive habits can land a person in a psychiatric hospital behind locked doors. And we routinely suspend the independence of children when lack of experience or imperfect self-control threatens them with harm.

Revealingly, when concern for life and pain conflicts with respect for liberty, our tendency is to surrender liberty. Laws criminalizing suicide and euthanasia show that we are reluctant to permit freedom to trump suffering. Patrick Henry may not have realized how radical he was in preferring death to a life without freedom; we admire his bold statement without being inclined to agree with it. Even soldiers fighting for their country's independence may not prefer death to loss of liberty, staying with their comrades only because desertion is likely to cause them more pain than the mere possibility of being killed or wounded. Legislators tend to be so intent on allaying suffering that in their deliberations they don't even take into account the loss of freedom caused by every law.

We can sensibly ask why liberty tends to take a backseat to welfare in our choices. As with anything significant, there are multiple causes. One is that freedom constitutes an unbridled, not reliably social element of human nature. It presents the unpredictable side of our fellows, leading to both admirable and abominable acts. Consisting in its broadest sense of acting on whatever idea comes into our heads, it is viewed as uniquely dangerous and in need of external control. A second reason for the subsidiary position of freedom may well be an asymmetry that makes room for hope. Surrendering liberty in order to alleviate suffering and secure life leaves us, it is supposed, with the possibility of regaining freedom, while insisting on the right to make our own decisions and choosing death puts a permanent end to all our quests. This is the attitude that was expressed in Bertrand Russell's famous motto "Rather red than dead." The problem with this approach is that it may lose us liberty irredeemably by sinking us into a comfortable life in which the very idea of self-determination comes to seem alien.

It may well be that the moral imagination itself is weaker in enabling us to appreciate the legitimacy of unimpeded action than in being mobilized by the contagion of immediate feeling. There may be evolutionary reasons for this. Viewing others as weak and requiring help contributes to social cohesion and action, offering distinct advantages for survival. The free activity associated with the "loner," by contrast, tends to be suspicious to the crowd and may lead to dangerous behaviors. This is probably what Friedrich Nietzsche had in mind in his account of the strong, self-determining individual, though the line he draws between the hero and the herd achieves too sharp a contrast. It may be more accurate to say that people tend to sympathize with the plight of their neighbors and also to value unimpeded decision making, although they find acting on the former easier and less disquieting than practicing the art of choice.

The asymmetrical strength of the two teachings of the moral imagination disappears when unwelcome interference crushes liberty. We seem not to know how highly we value being left alone until alien forces impinge on every choice. What Ralph Waldo Emerson called "self-reliance," the practice of gaining control over all of one's activities, is very difficult to achieve. Education, social pressure, the benefits of conformity, and the weight of habit all militate against finding our own way in the world. The task is made nearly impossible because in undertaking it, we can have no guide; to turn to another to show us how is the surest way to surrender self-reliance. Yet we mourn its absence when we find our actions narrowly controlled in a job or our choices arbitrarily restricted by government. Smoldering resentment of a greater power, anger at limits imposed by alien force, and frustration at the gulf between what we want and what we are permitted to do bring home the preciousness of being left alone. Suffering engages us by its presence; we value freedom most when it is gone.

Unsurprisingly perhaps, we find it easier to appreciate our own demand to be left alone than the desire of others to be free from our interventions. That others should let us operate untrammeled strikes us as self-evident. Are we not, after all, in a better position to know what we want and what is good for us than anyone else in the world? The call of others to be rid of our ministrations, by contrast, looks willful and unwise. Are we not, after all, older or smarter or more experienced or cooler in judgment or more foresightful than our friends?

Reaching parity between oneself and others is an exceptionally difficult moral task. How can we get people—ourselves included—to see that everyone's claim to freedom is equally legitimate? The more we fall in love with our own values and ideas, the more difficult this becomes. The only way to accomplish it is by the challenge of parity, which amounts to the question "How would I feel if I were in the other person's circumstances?" The challenge is more effective when applied to freedom than to such substantive values as drug use and financial success. Commitments to certain specific goals may be unintelligible to people; desires for alcohol and riches, for example, are baffling to some and elicit from them no sympathy. The craving to do as one wishes, on the other hand, has been felt by nearly everyone, so the challenge of parity falls on rich experiential soil.

Some philosophers deny the universal significance of self-motivating freedom. They say that moral action is incompatible with doing what we wish. True freedom for Immanuel Kant and others is to be bound by rules or principles so that we do not what we want, but what is right. One is tempted to say that calling duty "freedom" is an annoying obfuscation, but that does not go to the heart of the matter. The truth is the deeper insight that even doing our duty is an expression of our freedom because, as Russell and many others have pointed out, we would not do it unless we wanted to.

Recognizing the desire to be left alone to pursue one's purposes is the first great step toward respecting the freedom of others. The acknowledgment, however, is not enough. I once saw a man capture a beautiful moth and put it in a box to carry home. The creature threw itself desperately against the side of box, trying to liberate itself from death in captivity. The man recognized the desire for freedom but showed utter indifference to it. Perhaps he could not see himself in the situation of the moth; more likely, since it was not his situation, he simply did not care.

This suggests that the ultimate foundation of leaving others alone is caring for them. The desire of people to be free cannot be a matter of indifference to any of us. That in many parts of the world women are not permitted to make their own decisions, that the poor are disenfranchised, that members of some races are denied participation in social life, and that communicants of some religions are not permitted to worship as they choose are rightly matters of concern to us. Freedom and the attendant right to be left alone are fundamental features of personhood. Respect for the operational independence of individuals is respect for their humanity and their life.

What, then, are the reasons why people do not leave each other alone? If freedom or unimpeded individual operation is central to human fulfillment, why do so many of us go out of our way to rob others of it? The answer begins by noting that social life is immensely valuable to all of us; without it, we would not have been able to attain the control we exercise over the planet. The interventions of others into our activities constitute one of the painful costs of communal living. The desire for control appears to know no limits, driving people to disregard the distinction between human actions and natural events: they want to shape the one just as much as they exercise lordship over the other.

A part of the reason why we want control may be a sense of weakness or vulnerability that makes us see alternative ways of life as threats. But if this were all, the attainment of mastery would provide only relief. In fact, however, imposing one's will on other people serves as the source of a profoundly satisfying, positive pleasure. The delight is supported by the conviction that we know better than others what is natural and right and a feeling of benevolence at our willingness to share superior wisdom. The full engagement of our cognitive and emotional machinery makes it difficult to control the drive for control, and we end up trying to instruct the world in what it ought to do.

4

TELLING OTHERS WHAT TO DO

IN A POPULOUS society where expert information is fragmented and broadly distributed, it is natural, wise, and perhaps necessary to seek guidance from others. Physicians can offer useful advice about what to do when we are ill; lawyers are indispensable when writing contracts or defending oneself against suit. Priests and ministers have a right to prescribe how to worship in their churches, and it is appropriate for instructors to teach us how to write. These are legitimate cases of others telling us what to do, if only because we submit ourselves to their greater or special knowledge and skill.

There are also instances where overt consent is not required for others to have the authority to tell us what to do. Congress can decide how much we are to pay in taxes, and the police have the right to command us to move on. Parents are entitled to instruct their young children about appropriate behavior, and nations can warn other nations of the consequences of aggression. Even in commercial life, restaurants can demand that patrons wear jacket and tie, and bakers can tell us not to taste the bread before purchase.

The modern world operates largely by people telling one another what to do or at least setting parameters for what is permissible. The phenomenon of the consultant hired to improve our practices is a relatively recent invention; the vast increase in the number of efficiency experts points to our interest in improvement. The reason these are acceptable cases of intervention by others in our regular patterns is that, by authority or conferred right, it is their business to tell us what to do. Evidently, we have some residual freedom in such matters: we can either act on their suggestions and demands or take the consequences of not complying. And indeed we often view government regulations as unnecessarily heavy-handed and the recommendations of experts as useless.

There are so many people and agencies telling us what to do that often we feel overwhelmed by demands and regulations. Actions are prescribed for us with such stringency and our sphere of operations is circumscribed so narrowly that sometimes we forget the experience of freedom. Young children complain about all they have to do to meet the requirements of school and parents; adults with jobs have no time and energy to do what they want. If individuals knew the tens of thousands of laws and government-originated rules that shape their lives, they would feel paralyzed.

Yet such guidance and limitation of our actions are by no means the most annoying. Many of them recede to become background conditions of life, accepted as unavoidable and hardly noticed. We may even find comfort in the limits, as a bird does in its cage. The more grating cases of others telling us what to do are those in which friends or strangers take it upon themselves to instruct us about our good. Often people think they know what we need or ought to want better than we do. Sometimes their intentions are unobjectionable, meaning to safeguard us from what they suppose are dire consequences. On occasion they may even be right, warning us of overlooked but real danger. Nevertheless, almost all such verbal interference is perceived as unsolicited and unwelcome meddling.

Experiencing such interventions as unwelcome suggests a buried but active sense of human freedom. We are convinced that what we do is uniquely our business and that no one but the person doing it should have a say in it. This notion of the private ownership of one's decisions and acts is supported by the operational independence of biological organisms and the natural unity of human actions. The organism, making its plans and executing them, is normally adequate to perform the actions that may be desired or necessary, and the consequences of the act reside primarily with the agent. If two people decide to marry, for example, the plan, the action, and what follows pertain primarily to the interested parties. The good of others—family and friends—require to be taken into account, but the calculation need not go beyond the couple's private judgment. Unsolicited advice, warnings of danger, and outlines of alternatives are beyond the right of others to offer and hence inappropriate.

But, one can reasonably ask, what if one has important relevant information? What if one knows something damaging about the proposed partner's history, financial situation, or relatives? Would a friend not do an injustice to a friend by withholding knowledge of these facts? Friends acquire the right, and under certain circumstances the obligation, to share what they know only if they are asked. Should they wish to divulge information, therefore, they need to create opportunities to be asked, not in a way that hints at their special knowledge, but subtly or as is proper to a caring party. The question or the request to speak opens the door to a frank conversation. Without it, the only proper act is silence.

People who do not want to hear potentially damaging information have a right to their ignorance. This means, of course, that their marriage may face problems down the line, problems that perhaps could have been prevented. Freedom is a costly good, which is a fact well known but oft forgotten. The most costly exercise of freedom, Adam and Eve's disobedience in the Garden of Eden, reminds us that the ability to choose is at once the ability to choose the wrong thing. The biblical story carries a profound moral point: God could have arranged matters in such a way that evil would have held no attraction for the first couple. This, however, would have denied them genuine choice—that is, the self-determination without which there is no moral credit. We do not praise grass for growing in the spring or rocks for peaceful slumber on the ground. But we admire individuals who resist temptation, control their impulses, and make a habit of choosing what is right.

Individuals who, unasked, insist on sharing information tacitly claim to know what is good for others. This is a momentous conceit. We cannot know what people value without extensive familiarity with their inner lives, and such access is almost always denied us. Marriage partners after thirty years of attentive caring may come to know each other's likes and peculiarities; for the rest, we operate with stereotypes and hunches. It is impossible for an outsider to know how people who decide to marry value information. Some may want to examine family histories three generations back; others might insist on dealing with problems as they arise and letting everything come as a surprise. In the end, no one other than the agent is in a position to determine what is important for a person to know. Even in the case of serious medical conditions, some people prefer to know nothing and die rather than face their ailment.

The reticence and carefully guarded privacy of the stereotypical New Englander appear to have been replaced by an openness that invites interference and permits everyone to have their say. Internet social networking sites are both symptom and engine of this development. It seems to please people to reveal some of the most intimate details of their lives. Directed at their friends, and in some cases at the world at large, this serves as a request for commentary. The response often takes the form of friendly support or concrete suggestions. One can wonder how beaming oneself nude and vulnerable to an unlimited public contributes to one's self-respect, but to the extent that reaction to the image is sought and welcomed, one's freedom is not compromised. It does not take long, however, for responses to go beyond acceptable limits: hurtful suggestions of divorce, cruelty to family members, and bankruptcy can follow hard on the heels of messages of sympathy.

These are but special cases of interference disguised as benevolence. Other cases abound at work, at the grocery store, and even at the doctor's office, where strangers in the waiting room voice their opinions to strangers about how to improve their attitude and behavior. People do not hesitate to tell us how to control our children, how to gain more attention from our mates, and how to make our diet healthier. They stand ready to share ideas about which doctor to see, what pills to take, and how to lose weight. Judging by what they claim to know, people are walking encyclopedias of useful information. In reality, most of what they suggest is of little value. Based on narrow experience and lacking specialist knowledge, they reach out to let the world know how well-informed they are and to put their imprint on what others do.

Often it is difficult to escape these benevolent meddlers. They seem to be everywhere, telling us what to do and criticizing our habits and values. Self-controlled saints can, of course, overlook the unwanted ministrations, but the rest of us find it difficult not to get annoyed. Their claim to benevolence makes these spouts of wisdom invulnerable. If we respond to their opinions by saying that we are perfectly capable of taking care of our own affairs, they act hurt and assure us that they wanted only to help.

Is there a general principle on the basis of which we can determine when it is appropriate to share information or tell others what to do? There is such a rule, though without context and detail it tends to remain vacuous. In general, verbal interference in the affairs of others is legitimate under the double proviso that what is to be said is ours to convey and that relevant others desire to hear it. The first proviso excludes gossip, rumor, and innuendo; these are bits of intelligence not ours to share. The second forbids blurting things out, gaining the attention of people on false pretenses, and providing unsolicited advice; these are cases in which people have not shown themselves prepared to lend an ear.

The principle, however, is no more than a general guideline or indication of what verbal interference is acceptable. Sometimes, speaking is legitimate even though one of the two conditions is missing. Yelling at people to get out of the way of an unnoticed speeding car is justified even if they have not indicated that they are ready to listen. It may also be proper to share information even though it is not ours, as with telling individuals of nefarious plots directed against them. Notice that in both of these exceptions, the legitimating factor is potential harm or immediate danger. The danger must be palpable and the harm substantial, or else the affair becomes just another case of meddling. Using the pretext that their reputation is at stake in order to justify telling a young couple that a friend is saying nasty things about them strikes sensible people as a flimsy excuse for rumor mongering.

The situation is further complicated by the difficulty of knowing what constitutes harm for others. One can reasonably suppose that being crushed by cars is not part of the life plan of people, whereas reputational damage may be a matter of indifference. Yet we cannot be sure even of this much: the person under the wheels of the car may have got there because he wanted to collect insurance, while a thoroughly ruined reputation may well pave the way to a best seller. Obviously we must make some assumptions about what we can reasonably view as damage, but the staggering variety of human values suggests that all assumptions must be constantly monitored and questioned. The best way of communicating is to say little and to say it cautiously at the start, and watch for interest and willingness to hear more. How much should be said is thus a matter of judgment that requires both good sense and vigilance.

The self-control expressed in silence and in the readiness to stop in mid-sentence if it seems inappropriate to speak are thoroughly admirable character traits. Nevertheless, they may make us appear insufficiently sensitive to the feelings and needs of others. Isn't everybody entitled to know everything that pertains to them, after all? Is it not irresponsible to withhold information concerning how others feel about our friends and acquaintances or to fail to offer them helpful advice on how to live their lives? This is the benevolence gambit once again, permitting us to pretend that we are motivated solely by the good of others. The claim is untenable, however, because it makes the unwarranted assumption that we have vitally important and accurate information to share.

The facts fly in the face of this conceit. Strangers have no reason to believe that the information they offer is of value. Friends are likely to choose themselves as embodying the standard to which we should aspire. Older people tend to forget that circumstances have changed since they acquired their wisdom. Spouses ready to tell their partners what to do are bent on changing them, which is usually designed to promote their own interests. People who give advice lack specialist knowledge;

even specialists can deal only in generalities, rarely taking the time and often lacking the ability to penetrate the secrets of the private heart. The result is a world of talk, much of which is invasive and superficial.

Another way to look at verbal intervention is in terms of the relations of the parties involved. Some relations authorize, some demand, and some positively forbid sharing information. I can request, for example, that you tell me each time I make an error while learning French. This gives you blanket permission to stop me as I speak and administer correction. The request imposes no obligation, however: I cannot demand that you help me improve my skills. If, on the other hand, you are my French teacher, calling me on the carpet for errors becomes mandatory. Yet other relationships make the disclosure of information unacceptable, such as when a person confides in you or if you work for a company with trade secrets.

Life is made easier by the rules and relationships that forbid sharing information. People who have access to top secrets are expected not to divulge them. Priests must not tell what they hear in the confession booth. Information about the health problems of individuals is to be shielded from all unauthorized persons. Disclosure of generally unknown facts about a company may lead to insider trading, which is punishable as a crime. Car dealers feel they must hide their true costs, and chefs have to guard their recipes. In much of institutional life what may and what may not be said is clearly determined.

There is far less official guidance in the interactions of professionals with their clients. Doctors can use their discretion in what they tell their patients about their disease, and although the communications of lawyers are supposed to be truthful and accurate, they are unlikely to be complete. No precise rules govern how psychiatrists should communicate with their patients or ministers with their congregants. Bankers and mortgage brokers cannot be charged with being overly generous with information, and political operatives divulge their plans on a strict "need-to-know" basis.

The relationship between professionals and their clients points to the fact that often not too much but too little information is conveyed. This may occur because what needs to be said is too esoteric, because the client may be undereducated, or because the pressure of time makes detailed conversation impossible. In certain cultures, however, professionals make a point of hiding relevant facts from the people for whom they work. In much of Europe, for example, patients are sheltered from the diagnosis of fatal illness; their inquiries are deflected by empty assurances and paternalistic lies. This is a different vice from telling sundry people what to do. Instead of directing people when there is no need, here doctors fail to disclose knowledge vitally important to their patients.

The vice of providing too little information is remedied to a fault by the Internet, which acts as the repository of all useful and useless intelligence. Anyone who turns for guidance to this momentous warehouse of knowledge and misinformation is certain to come away confused. As in the rest of our lives, nothing on the Web is guaranteed. One good suggestion is annulled by a contradictory second one, and much of what claims to be time-tested and accurate truth turns out to be questionable or flawed. But consulting the Web is, at least, a voluntary effort that we can simply forego. Individuals with convictions about what we ought to know, on the other hand, tend to seek us out and deliver their opinions without regard to our needs or interest.

Bloggers act as the Web-based equivalents of people who buttonhole us to share their views of the world and to tell us what we ought to think and do. Because they present themselves as supremely self-assured and self-important, it is a shock to realize that many of these writers have little to say and they say it poorly. Education used to teach perspective: students learned what was of significance and what did not need to be remembered. It placed us in the midst of intellectual giants and did not permit the illusion that we were of much significance. Those days appear to be gone. With the aid of ready access to the Internet, anyone can memorialize any set of worthless experiences. This is one of the awful consequences of the new power to publish one's own writing, no matter how jejune, and thereby call attention to one's ideas, no matter how infantile.

Not so many years ago, publication required convincing other people that one's work had merit. This constituted a check on the apparently limitless appetite of people for self-display. Editors and publishers exercised two central powers: they brought good work to the attention of the public, and they suppressed the self-indulgent lucubrations of ordinary minds. The obstacle they represented was actually a vital safeguard so that people would not embarrass themselves by their simple ideas and inferior prose. Today, by contrast, anyone can start a blog and fill cyberspace with a torrent of ill-chosen words. Mundane experiences, incoherent reflections, and ignorant theories can be advertised to the world. Prejudices may be presented as considered judgments, and untutored feelings are permitted to seize the focus of attention.

Apparently there is no one to tell the offending bloggers to rethink and rephrase because what they produce is a draft in need of craft. The only thing that seems to matter is the satisfaction of the blogger, and people without standards are easily satisfied. If all this detritus survives, what will future generations think of the condition of the human mind in our day? Some bloggers act like literary versions of Dr. Frankenstein: they use publication to breathe life into malformed ideas. Even if people never had better thoughts than they have today, only a few of them ought to be preserved. The proper fate of the rest is to remain the private possession of uninteresting minds and to accompany their owners quietly to the grave. At the very least, they should not lie in wait to assault the unsuspecting surfer of the Internet with worthless chatter.

The institutional rules restricting what may be said and the practices governing the communication of professionals with their clients leave the ordinary interactions of individuals largely unaffected. Astonishingly, people feel no compunction in sharing their opinions about what others—even unknown others—ought to do. Are people so certain of the excellence of their ideas that they feel superior to those who are mired in the task of making up their minds? Do they simply not care about how their intervention is received, so that telling people becomes self-expression rather than communication? Or do they seek to give advice because it suggests that their own lives are in order?

Determining what motivates people to intervene in the lives of others is difficult, perhaps mainly because the offenders do not know it themselves. Further, they may not notice that their interference is objectionable, finding the reluctance of people to follow their suggestions baffling or the sign of inferior intelligence. Only in the rarest of cases do people push the mute button and cease the chatter. Development of the ability to speak has apparently unleashed a torrent of sound from the human throat and made the desire to talk irresistible. We are so devoted to voicing feelings and ideas that in the absence of listeners we talk to ourselves, surrounding our actions with exclamations and explanations. We talk so much that even the animals that live with us learn to make sounds in an attempt to communicate.

The benefits of verbal communication are immense: complex coordinated activities, on which civilized life depends, would be impossible without it. The general intelligibility of language and the precise signification it makes possible are difficult to match. But talk is at its best when it directs action or takes the form of mutual exchange. Informing others of what they do not wish to hear is language in overdrive and hardly escapes the status of chatter. Yet such prattling seems thoroughly satisfying to some people who do not mind converting speech—once said to be a gift from the gods—into an instrument of nuisance and nastiness. The invention of the telephone vastly expanded the circle of those who can be informed and commanded about, and the precipitous drop in the cost of communication as a result of computers and the Internet removed the last obstacle to haranguing the entire world through email, social networking pages, Listservs, and blogs.

What can we do to restrain this flow of words? The first line of defense must be inattention. Not listening to uninvited talk is the mighty privilege of all. If the offenders are near, we cannot stop the sound waves they generate from penetrating our ears. But it is easy not to listen to what they say or to convert their words into something that sounds like the twitter of birds. A benign look might convey the undesired impression that we hear and heed what they are saying, so it may be best to look into the distance with impassive face. The advantage of this approach is that, without giving overt offense, it dries up the river of words after a while.

Those who prefer more direct and decisive action may simply announce that they wish to hear none of it. Telling people that we are not interested in their information or instructions may sound abrupt, but it should not be considered an insult. Since the ethics of communication is violated by uninvited chatter, indicating a desire for the speaker to stop may sound impolite, but is in fact only self-defense that reestablishes the balance of silence. There is little need to go on a campaign to strike out at the offenders; it is better to pity them in the quiet of our souls for their desperate need to talk and to flood the world with their ideas.

One strategy of dealing with excess verbiage works for suggested actions but not for information. Self-confident people can afford to listen to a host of ideas about what they ought to do without losing command of their lives. Some of the suggestions may actually have merit, so hearing them out can expand alternatives and call for judgment. Listening to what people say but reserving decision for oneself can serve a useful function in self-improvement. On the other hand, we cannot open our ears to rumor and innuendo and then dismiss as irrelevant the nasty things we heard. We do not have to be Othello to find the well poisoned by what others say so that—perhaps unconsciously—our actions come to reflect the damaging information. For this reason it is better to stop listening to gossip the moment it begins to flow.

The prevalence of gossip is supported by the gigantic machinery of communication in our society. Some publications are devoted exclusively to the propagation of damaging information about people, but even daily newspapers report "dirt" concerning the powerful and the famous. Radio and television programs, blogs and Listservs vie with one another to break stories and thereby to get credit for their keen discernment of human folly. Photographers rush about to document trysts or to catch politicians and movie stars in their moments of embarrassment. The revelations are greeted with mock outrage by the public as people declare that their worst suspicions have been confirmed.

Those who expose infidelity, corruption, duplicity, and incompetence lay claim to a grand moral justification of their revelations. Is it not an important public service, after all, to show the moral failings of admired individuals? And is it not appropriate that we should take delight in the destruction of unearned reputations? Information about the private nastiness of the beautiful and the mighty assures us that no one is better than anyone else, that human nature throbs with the same cravings everywhere. This is a useful thing to remember, but it falls short of a wholesale justification of gossip. The reason is that the activity of exposing folly also displays a morally disgraceful side: it legitimates the idea that human nature is irredeemably flawed and denies us the benefit of shining exemplars who can serve as models for our lives. Its focus on the nasty in human existence distorts the facts, and, worse, it fosters the thoroughly objectionable trait of taking pleasure in other people's pain.

In reflecting on the quantity of communication in our lives, we may be tempted to call ours a "talk society." This, however, is only one side of the coin. The other calls attention to all the things we do not talk about. Many of these should be openly discussed but for one reason or another are kept under wraps. The desire for secrecy is easy to understand in private matters: few people want to see details of their married life broadcast to the public. The growing availability of sex tapes documenting what used to be private activities in the bedroom does not diminish the continuing demand to be left alone. The difference is that the display of sexual prowess adds to one's fame or self-image, whereas public discussions of one's family problems serve only as an embarrassment. Small wonder, then, that the former is widely disseminated while the latter remains largely unmentioned or unacknowledged.

Secrecy becomes problematic when it concerns the public's business. Matters relating to national security are properly kept secret, as are the health records of private citizens. But qualifications for government posts, the reasons for regulations, proposed legislation and the arguments for it, along with explanations of what is behind the actions bureaucrats take to promote the public good should be open to all interested parties. The ability to see the rules by which one's society operates as one's own is essential for compliance and for the sense that one is at home in the world. Knowing the practices of the community and understanding the need or the reasons for them constitute indispensable conditions of such appropriation.

What we find instead is voluntary ignorance of governmental regulations and reluctance on the part of officials to disclose the purposes of their rules. This creates the impression that how a society operates is the business of politicians and civil servants rather than of everyone. The culture of secrecy makes it difficult for people to acquire the information that can serve as the foundation of critique, adding to the power of bureaucrats and leaving their discretion unchecked. It reinforces the habit of letting hirelings make vital decisions about the fate of the community, trusting that they (or some people somewhere) know what they are doing. This habit has become so deep-seated that, outrageously, legislators no longer read the gigantic bills their staffs produce and vote for or against them on the basis of cursory briefings and party demands.

Democratic self-determination means that the community proposes, discusses, and eventually decides what to do and then does it. To the extent that individuals within the community surrender their decision-making power, they allow others to tell them what to do and thereby to take over their lives. The resulting death of activity is at once the loss of freedom: safe passivity takes the place of the risk choice always involves. Of course, at its fringes the comfort shades into the feeling that we are being manipulated. As a result, although people surrender themselves to the architects of the community, they do so with quiet resentment. The anger grows to a destructive level when

individuals realize that often their elected leaders are only fig-
ureheads and the power resides in the hands of faceless execu-
tive assistants and Congressional staffs.

The growth of specialization and the veneration of exper-
tise reduce people to a level of significant personal insecurity.
They feel their knowledge is so deficient that they cannot trust
their choices and should make no decisions without specialist
advice. Before the arrival of certified advisors, individuals con-
sulted oracles, psychics, fortune tellers, and tarot card readers.
Once people realized that a comfortable living can be made
from telling others what to do, they formed guilds, established
criteria of certification, and imposed examinations on would-
be practitioners. As a result we can now enjoy the services of
financial advisors, psychological counselors, dieticians, interior decorators, personal trainers, marriage counselors, publi-
cists, service advisors, makeup artists, and life coaches. There
is hardly an area of life that has not been colonized by people
who are prepared, for a fee, to tell us what to do. Though experts
can be as wrong as the rest of us, they convey an aura of self-
assurance, and the fact that they charge for what they say seems
to legitimate their edicts to the public mind. The self-reliance
whose scarcity Emerson bemoaned in the nineteenth century
seems to have altogether disappeared in the twenty-first.

I have noted earlier that unsolicited advice offered by friends
and strangers can simply be disregarded. Expert advice, on the
other hand, can be limited by refusing to pay for it. Obviously
there are times and fields in which some help can be valuable;
in the case of serious illness, for example, we certainly want to
be under the care of good physicians. But much of what we normally need to know can be found in books and online, and the
most important elements in our decisions—our values—are
known by us better than they can be known by anybody else.
Body and mind constituting a person act as a single sensorium

that registers the worth of every experience. In the nature of the case, no one can instruct us concerning what we hold dear, and no one can gauge the depth of our devotion. It is perfectly appropriate, therefore, for each of us to make our own decisions about what to do with our money, how to run our lives, and whom to choose as friend or marriage partner. This is not a plea for ignorant decision making, but a call to take charge of our lives so that we may discover what we really want.

In addition to talk that is self-expressive or meant to instruct, there is also a kind that enables people to do things they could not otherwise undertake. When physicians tell us what we ought to do to maintain or regain health, the talk is designed to convey information and perhaps to outline courses of action. But they also order medications, telling the pharmacist which drugs to dispense. Such orders create access to chemicals we would normally not be able to obtain. The entire system of prescription drugs operates on the basis of the restriction of human freedom: we are judged incompetent to decide which medications we want to try, and the decision is handed, paternalistically, to our doctors. What they say we can have is made available to us; without prescription, the drug cannot be obtained. The doctor's word creates reality.

Although prescribing medications is telling us what to do, we retain control over our lives by deciding whether we wish to buy or to take them. Nevertheless, physicians exercise significant power over us in having the availability of drugs dependent on their word. Their authority limits our freedom and makes it impossible for us to do many of the things we want. The argument for the monopoly power of the medical profession over drugs is that without their protection we would likely harm ourselves. This rationale suggests that God should have harvested the apples of the forbidden tree in the Garden of Eden before Adam and Eve got there and put them under lock and key. Of course, we can harm ourselves by experimenting with chemicals whose properties we do not fully understand, but no more so than by choosing the wrong mate or the wrong profession. That, however, is an argument for education, not for external control. Because humans are by nature inquisitive experimenters, protecting them from themselves is the shortest road to tyranny. Denying adults access to the means of action is an illegitimate restriction of their operations. It bridges the gap between telling others what to do and forcing them to do what they don't want. It goes beyond verbal criticism and admonishment but succeeds only in setting limits to what can be done, without decisive influence over positive action. By making it impossible for people to act on their desires, it robs them of an essential element of their freedom.

5

MAKING OTHERS DO WHAT WE WANT (AND THEY DON'T)

THE OPERATIONAL INDEPENDENCE of human beings gives them the sense that they can do, without aid, whatever must be done to sustain life and to satisfy it. This, of course, is an illusion that rapidly disappears when the world takes an unfavorable turn or they encounter powerful alien forces. But even if there are special times when help is needed, humans and other animals tend to retain the desire to be left alone so they can operate without interference. This hankering for freedom is not an accidental or dispensable feature of living creatures. On the contrary, we see it even in babies and in sick elderly people, in domesticated animals no less than in those living in the wild.

The focus of the drive for freedom is bodily integrity and unimpeded motion. Its motive resides in the will that begins to define from birth what the organism wants and how it aims to obtain it. The will is fierce in its self-determination, fighting interference with every muscle and all the tools at its disposal. Children who can hardly speak say "I, I," indicating the desire to perform the task without help, alone. Many adults feel cheated if others remove a challenge or relieve them of the need to perform a favored activity. Most of us are devoted not only to our choice of things to do but also to our manners of performing them: how we chew our food, drive a car, and fall asleep are treasured peculiarities.

One might think that the desire to control their own fates would keep people sufficiently occupied to leave others alone. At the very least, they could be expected to have developed universal sympathy for all things that toil for independence, viewing the necessary interference in their lives when we have to fight them, use them, or eat them as a tragic flaw in the design of the universe. That, however, is not the way we operate. The will is not satisfied with running its own affairs; it wants to gain power over others and control its small corner of the world. The evils that come from this desire for control define the history of the human race. Slavery, the cruel treatment of women and minorities, the persecution of strangers, and the exploitation of children connect directly to the drive to crush other wills. The fact that someone else wants something is often reason enough to make its attainment difficult or impossible.

A study of the psychology of the will may show that its urge to establish supremacy is an outcome of its weakness. The powers of the self are sharply limited, and the world is constantly and dangerously changing. To stabilize change is to reduce one's vulnerability; to eliminate the different is to make the universe safer and closer to being a home. Thus we find struggles in the family; among rivals; between classes, races, and nations; and between adherents of different religions. A clever commercial announces, "Have it your way," offering what sounds like victory over circumstance and contingency. There is no problem in making this generous offer in the choice of hamburgers, but very few people are ready to surrender control over things that matter. The restaurants behind the ad do not want customers to determine the price, the size, and the quality of their product;

they yield only concerning such indifferent issues as whether a hamburger should be served with pickles.

When it comes to matters that matter, we want things our way and not anyone else's. This is how, paradoxically perhaps, the source of our desire for liberty becomes the greatest danger to liberty; each of us wants freedom to rule, which can be achieved only by denying freedom to others. Leaving others alone is a great virtue because it amounts to recognition of the equal right of all to self-determination. To take it seriously we must surrender our desire to crush or dominate others and get out of the way when people want to chart their own course. The best response to the efforts of others to find meaning in their lives is to cheer them on. Under certain circumstances it is appropriate to aid them, but at the very least we should not present an obstacle to their independence.

Admittedly some people place little value on freedom. The measure of this is not how they relate to some grand ideal, but rather their feelings about control of their daily activities. Some years ago I had a student who upon graduating from college rushed to join the army. He told me that he did not want to make decisions; he wanted someone else to tell him when to get up, what to eat, and how to organize his day. We see the same pattern in some cultures in which women subject themselves to the rule of men and men to the edicts of religious leaders. True believers in ideologies also tend to surrender their freedom because they are naïve enough to think that a few simple ideas, as interpreted by charismatic leaders, can explain everything and provide adequate guidance for life.

It should not go without notice, however, that total surrender of freedom is rare and may not even be possible. Women who live at the mercy of men retain a certain amount of independence: they raise the children and control many of the daily routines of home life. Religions and ideologies may determine the outlines of existence, but they rarely penetrate to its details. People who live under their sway tend to hold on to decision power over whom to wed, which approved foods to eat, and when and how to perform the necessary functions of biological and social life. Even my student who joined the army complained that not enough of his daily existence was regimented—he could not avoid at least a small measure of self-determination.

People who want to surrender their freedom tend to view the prospect of making wrong decisions as terrifying. Some of them believe that others are able to do a better job than they can of determining what they should value and what they should do. Others among them find that choosing is a burden they want to escape. They believe they can achieve satisfaction only by becoming drones that never worry about anything in life. Such servitude, however, is voluntary and retains a modicum of the pleasure that accompanies free activity. Likely it would not be enjoyed if the context were slavery or forcible separation from those they love.

Although organisms are operationally independent, they cannot live without the cooperation of their fellows. Parents bring them into the world, friends defend them, partners help render their days meaningful, and untold numbers of unknown others join with them to create and operate the institutions of social life. The idea that the individual, if left alone, enjoys absolute freedom is a fiction of political philosophers. It is a dream or an abstraction, because we cannot live long and well if we live alone, and if there had been no others, we would not be alive at all. The seventeenth-century British philosopher Thomas Hobbes spoke of the initial absolute freedom of the individual, but even he knew that in a social context many of those freedoms must be surrendered. Living with others requires at least that we refrain from killing them and taking their property.

Such limitations of freedom are adopted freely. Realizing that theft and murder are not good strategies, sensible people restrain themselves from committing them. This is the morally most acceptable method of reining in liberty, because it is not a loss of it to someone else. In such situations people retain both their desire for a particular action and their ability to perform it but, in light of the consequences, freely decide to pass. The combination of understanding and self-control necessary for this are hallmarks of the foresightful, civilized person—someone who respects the rights of others and accommodates them in a shared world. Free decisions not to exercise one's freedom yield a uniquely satisfying pleasure; although the delight of release is missing in them, the knowledge that release was possible but forgone can greatly elevate one's self-respect.

Since freedom is the ability to do what we want, there are two other, far less acceptable ways that we can trim its sails: we can try to eliminate antisocial desires, and we can curtail the power to act on them. In our society we try to teach children to find violence so repulsive that they do not even feel tempted by it. When the lessons work, they crush destructive cravings; it simply does not occur to well-raised young people to kill or maim their neighbors. Their power to cause harm is disabled by lack of desire, and they never get the feeling that their freedom is compromised. Are they in fact free? Not at all, for two connected reasons. They are robbed of desire, which is a vital ingredient of freedom, and they are denied opportunity for moral growth in freely surrendering their aggressive impulses.

The idea of manipulating people's desires points the way to frightful dystopias. Aldous Huxley's *Brave New World* comes to mind, with its shameless engineering of desires to make them fit the stations and conditions of its people. Behavior psychologist B. F. Skinner's *Walden Two* presents a superficially more benign picture, even though one need not look far to realize that here, too, a simulacrum of happiness takes the place of freedom. These, however, are older efforts to explore the possibilities of mind control; these authors would be astonished to learn of the techniques of brainwashing and the power of deep brain stimulation that have been developed since their day. Before long, the rapidly expanding sciences of the brain may offer governments the opportunity to create compliant and smiling people who, although their feelings and thoughts are engineered, nevertheless believe that they are free.

The second way of controlling the antisocial manifestations of freedom operates by restricting the ability of people to act on their desires. This can occur by the outright removal of instruments necessary to do damage to each other. For example, the government can collect all the firearms in a society or place harmful drugs under the supervision of authorized individuals. It can also be accomplished by threats of speedy and severe punishment, as in the cases of fraud and the molestation of children. Until recently these have been the major and possibly only methods of keeping the exercise of freedom within limits. They require negative reinforcements supported by the overwhelming power of the state.

Over the centuries the attempt to control human beings has not diminished in scope and intensity. The only major improvement is that instead of the arbitrary decrees of a king or nobleman, we face the well-articulated and supposedly evenhanded demands of a central authority. This may make for greater justice and transparency but not for less need of self-control. If anything, there are many more restrictions on freedom today than there have ever been. Nearly every area of our lives is governed by laws. The sheer number of people surrounding us requires extensive rules of interaction, and every regulation takes a toll on self-determination. The truth of the claim that our freedom is severely restricted and continues to erode can be observed all around us every day.

When people are free, they can do what they want. They lose that freedom when others make them do what *they* want. This occurs in three separate but related ways: (1) individuals near or dear demand certain actions, (2) social customs structure and limit our behavior, and (3) laws require much that we are disinclined to do. People we care for are constantly in the business of shaping our activities. Over an adjustment period that lasts as long as the marriage, spouses make each other behave as they wish. Husbands are taught to limit watching football and not to forget anniversaries; wives may be required to stay within the budget and not to discuss marital relations with their girlfriends. Parents catalog a host of actions they will not permit their children to perform. Children, in turn, sigh and roll their eyes to make their elders lay off. Neighbors visit to complain about the dogs being too loud and off the leash; distant relatives show dissatisfaction with the meals they are served when they arrive unannounced. Everyone wants to correct somebody—and some people, as many as they can.

The informal shaping, conditioning, influencing, and controlling of humans begins in early childhood and continues throughout life. Children feel that most adult demands are external impositions they want to resist. They reject some of them because they interfere with playtime or don't promise fun; they shrink from others simply because their source is alien. From time to time, parents complain that the only way they can get their children to do something is by telling them *not* to do it. Though overstated, this contains an element of truth, and lovers of freedom readily understand why. In childhood and old age, people are reduced to the lowest levels of self-determination. Apart from the opportunity for play, itself provided by adults at their discretion, children's lives do not belong to them. Parents constitute powerful forces whose demands, backed by threats and the mayhem of punishments, make young people feel not in charge of their days.

Parents, for their part, experience pleasure when ruling over their children and consider demolishing their desires as a way to build character. Adversity does, indeed, contribute to strength of will, and the unloving actions of parents tend to add to the resilience of young souls. But early frustration augments desire and creates hatred of alien wills, leading to possibly lifelong friction within the family. Children of such parents may grow up thinking that the world aims to thwart their efforts and learn to view all others, strangers and pets included, as wishing them ill.

Instead of creating strong characters, overbearing parents succeed only in embittering their brood. The frustration receives reinforcement from teachers who consider learning a severe demand instead of the joyous activity it can be. The awful hours sitting quietly in class doing what the teacher requires further aggravate the suspicion that life consists of having to please others and abandoning even a vestige of self-determination. For some, college represents the first possibility of freedom, which young people celebrate by excesses of drinking, sex, and the violation of official requirements.

The cycle completes itself in marriage, where even the most reasonable desires of the mate cause resistance because they are read as alien demands. Those who do not enter professions, such as medicine and law, that permit significant self-determination must deal with a succession of bosses imposing undesirable tasks to be completed by hateful deadlines. The suffering of the people who make our institutions work remains a matter of conjecture only for those who fail to pay attention. But everyone knows that job satisfaction is possible only by acquiescing in established power relations. Bosses have to be pleased all day by doing what they want, and meeting the demands of spouse and children occupies the evening. Working people live with the feeling that very little of the week is reserved as their own in which they are free to do what they want and not what someone else desires.

In the modern world, bureaucrats surround us and discharge their frustration by subjecting their clients to arbitrary decisions or crushing indifference. They treat the people over whom they have temporary power as "cases" represented by files, with no attention to the longing and need they reveal. The deeply disquieting feature of dealing with "officials" is that although they are clearly human beings, they rarely permit themselves to show human emotions. From the standpoint of individuals, everyone is an exception, yet representatives of large institutions acknowledge no special condition or urgent cause. Everything is done according to rules and accomplished not by feeling humans, but by functionaries who view themselves as occupying roles. They have a "job" to do, and they do it the way bakers force dough into cookie-cutter shapes.

Officials make demands on everyone who enters their sphere of authority. They, on the other hand, have no direct obligation to their clients; they believe they owe allegiance only to the organization that pays them. Their decisions and actions are "nothing personal," revealing a mechanical approach to handling people that makes dealing with institutions infuriating. In the experience of many, there is little discernible difference between the machines that first answer the phone at large companies and the humans who eventually, often reluctantly, take over from them. The machines cannot handle anything out of the ordinary; too often, human operators won't. Their trump card takes the form of the ultimate excuse that they "only work here," suggesting that they, too, are impotent victims of a faceless system.

The unresponsiveness of institutions and their representatives, however, does not enable individuals to respond to them with matching indifference. Comfortable lives require large organizational structures. Water, electricity, heat, phone and Internet connection, food, and transportation all presuppose huge systems whose demands must be met and whose bills have to be paid by final deadlines. These institutions make us live by their rules, allowing little deviation from what they determine as routine. The adjustment, therefore, is altogether one-sided: individuals must fall in line and do what is required, while institutions can operate largely without taking the complaints of their clients into account. The official credo of large companies tends to assert the opposite of this reality, declaring that the customer is king. The operational procedures of institutions, however, give this claim the lie, forcing both employees and clients into its favored modes of behavior.

There is yet another way we can make others do what would normally never occur to them. Remarkably, the method of this influence is free from force and threat and presents itself as a way to enrich choice. The best example of this sort of process is advertising, which presumably does no more than present alternatives and invite preference. Thoughtful people hold widely divergent opinions on advertising—one group denouncing it as a nefarious attempt to manipulate people and another praising it as an appropriate way to acquaint us with opportunities. There are no doubt important differences between inviting people to drink a certain brand of beer and forcing them to buy and consume it; choice is not impaired by adding to one's knowledge. The informational function of advertising is therefore legitimate and harmless. But effective advertising does more than call attention to the availability of activities and goods; it attempts to create desires to obtain them. Since freedom is the ability to do what we want, calling cravings into existence is a subtle way of trying to make us do things. The new hungers tend to crowd out established desires and thereby limit, as they expand, the organ of choice.

Further, desires could not be created without making the use and possession of certain goods highly attractive. This is accomplished by associating them, often falsely, with the glamour of beauty, prosperity, and popularity. In this way advertising relies on and supports the conventional values of society. It presents people who are happy buying insurance, beautiful because they use facial creams, and satisfied with life if they can drink a couple of beers. Absurd as the associations may be, they contribute to making people want to be like others, suppressing interest in self-determination.

The second pressure on doing what we want derives from the unannounced but well-established practices of society. People cannot go to work in dirty clothes, no matter how desperate they are to feel relaxed. Fast-food restaurants offer no silverware and so make us eat like uncouth beasts. In some contexts it is unacceptable to broach the truth: we cannot tell our friends that they look terrible, our bosses that they are hateful, and our bankers that they act as greedy frauds. Those who ask why we would want to hurt other people by saying such things miss the point. Perhaps we would never say them if we could, but the fact that we cannot—that for many it is unthinkable to violate what society expects—makes the desire to do so all the more intense.

Informal social expectations influence our lives and likes profoundly and in ways we hardly notice. This should not surprise us. We grow up with them, rebel against them in the teenage years, and then settle into an existence defined largely by social customs. In doing so we exercise a certain amount of choice. Up to a point, we can decide on a profession, select a mate, and move to a part of the country we love. But the decisions are within limits set by convention; people do not marry zebras, no matter how intelligent and kind, and they make a living without offering torture and black magic for sale. The subterranean power of what others do and what they expect us to imitate is so great that we find ourselves mouthing the opinions and performing the rituals of the crowd.

Such conformity provides the comfort of belonging and eliminates the stigma of being different. There are at least two other reasons why compliance and uniformity rule. Actions set examples and can quickly become contagious, propelling us to do what others do or assume our parts in large-scale social acts. This occurs not only in panics and mob action but also in the imitation of admired individuals, such as sport heroes and movie stars. The world is full of little replicas of "the beautiful people" and of clothes, mannerisms, and actions thoughtlessly copied. The psychology of what looking and acting like famous individuals does for ordinary people has not been adequately studied.

The second reason for uniformity is that divergence from it draws comment, censure, and eventually punishment. Many of the goods of life are denied to those who fail to conform. Employment, companionship, friendship, even decent treatment tend to be unavailable to people who stray far from the norm. Women who fail to shave their armpits make others stare, men with beards to their chests need not look for a career in corporations, individuals without a known address arouse the suspicion of the police, and people who claim to be prophets end up in psychiatric institutions. We distrust people with foreign accents, avoid those who voice strange desires, and refuse contact with anyone whose behavior is unpredictable. In ordered societies, social customs are so successful in shaping behavior that laws seem hardly needed.

The power of social exemplars is great because they invisibly surround us from cradle to grave. Whether they like it or not, parents serve as models for their children. Schools extol the excellence of patriots, suggesting to students that George Washington, Susan B. Anthony, or Martin Luther King Jr. might provide guidance in their efforts to establish identity. Newspapers and magazines write with admiration about heroic ordinary people, the exploits of sport heroes, and the fortunes made by the fortunate few. Responsibility and reliability serve as defining virtues that earn success in life, and television shows, even those about odd people, depict only lovable and forgivable peculiarities.

Finally, there is a profusion of laws, each backed by the might of the city, state, or federal government, and they constitute the third source of our loss of freedom. In highly organized communities, government has a monopoly on power, retaining for itself the right to establish standards of behavior, mediate conflicts, and create and enforce regulations. Every law is an abridgement of freedom; each is a way of making others do what we want. One can reasonably ask who is included in the "we" that determines what people can and what they must not do. The standard answer identifies the "we" that make the laws as all the citizens of a nation. This, however, is clearly not the case in societies large enough to require representative government; in them, laws are formulated and installed by elected politicians. Since there is always a division of opinion among citizens about important matters, politicians cannot represent everybody's views. They act, presumably, on behalf of the good—as they conceive it—of the entire community. Whether that conception captures reality is difficult to determine and, in any case, may become clear only in the long run. What registers with great power and immediacy is that a few people in the city council, the state legislature, Congress, and federal rule-making agencies impose all manner of demands on all of us.

Some of the laws are unquestionably necessary and beneficial. The development of the criminal code was one of the towering moral achievements of the human race. Security of person and possessions is essential for a satisfying life. Although it involves a limitation of freedom, the burden of controlling our actions is shared by all: no one is permitted to kill or maim or rob another. Such laws are justified not only by the good they do and harm they forestall but also because what they protect is an essential condition of all freedom. There is no liberty without life or if actions are framed under the shadow of intimidation.

There is another set of laws justified by the fact that ours is a populous society. In a world of small communities and distant farms, people might not get in each others' way. They would pursue their lives protected by the criminal law and would hardly ever need central regulation. Matters are vastly different when interstate commerce moves vast quantities of goods from coast to coast and millions of automobiles hurry from city to city. To protect the public, drivers have to be tested and some authority must establish the rules of the road. Responsibilities have to be clarified, systems of enforcement established, and agencies of control funded. As a result, in getting on the highway drivers may feel that faceless others make them do what they do not want or set limits to their actions. I may wish to drive on the left side of the road or at a hundred miles an hour, travel without the benefit of lights at night, or decide to park in the middle of the road. Such bits of freedom are rightly limited to avoid chaos and slaughter. We may be annoyed at what feel like arbitrary rules, but although some elements of the rules are arbitrary (think speed limits), it is clear that a measure of order must be preserved.

However, the criminal code and laws necessary to preserve order in a populous society represent only a small portion of the regulations devised to command our actions. Congress and agencies of the federal government pass more than ten thousand rules and regulations having the force of law each year. There are laws that most people do not even know exist. Regulations reach into every sphere of life, telling us what we have to do and how. Forty-seven years ago, when I started teaching at my current institution, it had one part-time attorney to make sure it was in compliance with state and federal standards. Today, it has a large office full of lawyers interpreting the demands of the three busily regulating branches of the federal government. Admissions, financial aid, student privacy, campus security, access to buildings, equity between men and women in sports, employment decisions, and a hundred other practices are scrutinized to make sure they are in line with what central authority demands. Individuals do not escape the inclusive and intrusive rules framed by others; throughout our lives, on pain of fines or jail, we are expected to meet standards of behavior imposed by government.

Legislative bodies justify the laws they pass by reference to the public good. If this were an honest claim, most laws would be installed experimentally and monitored carefully to make sure they truly promote justice, safety, or happiness. Such studies are done, however, only on rare occasions; for the greatest part, laws are passed on flimsy evidence of their efficacy and tend to remain on the books indefinitely. Legislators pay strikingly little attention to how their acts affect liberty; they proceed as if new laws represented costless benefits. In reality, of course, every compulsory rule infringes freedom, and liberty is a vital element of the public good. Clearly, therefore, the most advocates of large-scale legislation can claim is that laws enhance the public good at the expense of diminishing it. In the case of each new law, we can—and should—appropriately ask if it will create more good by regulating conduct than existed in the form of freedom prior to regulation.

Meddlesome laws are perceived by people as others making us do what we do not want to do. This perception reveals their essence: however well meant, they are acts of some people imposing their will on others. Elected representatives are delegated the power to do this, but the art of politics consists in limiting the exercise of that power to cases that truly involve the public good and do not abolish private rights. The key requirement of a unified community is that citizens not think their leaders constitute an alien force. John Stuart Mill was right that legislation intruding on the private lives of individuals is inappropriate—that there are some subjects about which government should simply have no say.

As an example of poorly thought out legislative and judicial positions, consider life-and-death decisions by the very old and the very ill. There is a rising chorus of protest from sick elderly people over the legal obstacles in the way of assisted suicide. The ostensible reason for banning such practices is the interest of the state in human life. Defending people from the assault of others is a worthy task, but protecting them from their own considered judgments is absurd. No one is in a better position to determine if life has served its purpose than the individual whose life it is. If the decision to terminate life is made calmly and in consideration of the relevant facts, government—since it does not own that life—needs to remain on the sidelines. The Oregon experiment in legalizing euthanasia has demonstrated that the fear of mass suicides is ungrounded. Just as we do not have to make eating mandatory to keep people from starving themselves to death, so we do not have to force them to stay alive in order to make suicide unattractive. For the most part, people love to live, and it is unseemly for those who have not felt the pain of others to tell them that they have not had enough. Legislators show an amazing naiveté about the power of their regulations. They think they are clever in passing laws that leave no loopholes or exceptions, forgetting that thousands of lawyers will study each bill to counteract its intentions and subvert its meaning. It may take Congress months to craft a law; it takes smart individuals only a couple of hours to figure out a way around it. If legislators had a higher opinion of the average citizen, they would understand that the enforcement of laws is no substitute for voluntary compliance. Only free submission to the laws guarantees results, and that is impossible to gain so long as people perceive regulation as others making them do things against their will. The inefficiency and eventual collapse of the Soviet Union were occasioned largely because its people could not perceive its aims and laws as their own. Clever avoidance and surly resistance will bring any power to its knees.

6

HELPING OTHERS

THE MODERN WORLD is organized in such a way that people aid their fellows without intending to do so. Complex social acts such as raising, distributing, and marketing food can be performed only by the cooperation of large numbers of individuals. Those contributing to the act need not, and typically do not, think of their work as helping or benefiting others. They simply do their jobs: they perform certain activities and are paid for them. They might even suppose that they are the sole beneficiaries of their labors. In reality, however, they can profit only if others do, as well: economic arrangements are such that everyone contributes and all enjoy wholesome results.

This deeply moral structure of commercial life escapes many people precisely because it does not feature benevolent intentions. Actions within it require the efforts of countless individuals and, when all goes well, shower benefits on the participants. Commercial exchanges affirm the freedom of the parties involved and meet human needs; the clothes on my back, the heat in the house, and the food on the table are testimony to what others do for me. Of course, they require money for their services which, in turn, I earn by doing things for others. The system functions as a benign machine whose parts are coordinated to maximize the good.

The commercial world that envelops and nourishes all of us requires no intention on the part of those working within it beyond keeping a job and taking care of themselves. As a result, we don't normally think of it as an arena in which people help each other. Instead, we reserve the notion of help for application to cases where financial exchanges fail to meet human needs, such as those of abandoned children, sick people who cannot hold down jobs, and retirees who outlive their resources. People in such circumstances need the help of others and receive it as the result of individual kindness or organized charity. Here, intentions predominate: aiding others is a matter of individual decision on the basis of principle or inclination.

In some situations, leaving others alone and not helping them is both illegal and immoral. Letting paralyzed persons perish in a burning house and justifying it by saying we were respecting their right to be left alone is a grotesque distortion of our proper relation to others and their autonomy. People who believe in taking over the lives of those less fortunate depict the desire to let others operate unimpeded as socially irresponsible and insensitive to need. Nothing could be further from the truth. To leave others alone is not to abandon them, but to permit them to lead their lives by their own lights. When they need help, fellow humans must come to their aid and ease them over the hurdles they cannot clear alone.

Leaving others alone, therefore, is perfectly compatible with providing aid to the needy. The biblical injunction not to let our hearts harden amounts to a deeply significant moral principle. Perhaps as a result of the wealth humans have attained, we support the fallen among us: we feed starving millions around the globe, care for dementia patients in nursing homes, and cannot find it in our hearts to turn off the respirators of people in persistent vegetative states. We labor so others may live, sustaining people vastly beyond their productive years. Our generosity extends even to animals, financing shelters for them and making sure that marine mammals, Chinese brown bears, and mustered-out circus elephants lead safe and satisfying lives.

A problem donors face is how to give without attaching onerous conditions to their kindness. In giving money to beggars on the corner, many people want to make sure they don't use it for beer. Food stamps, an organized system of help, cannot be used to purchase cigarettes. Religious charities require that the individuals they help use the right words to pray to the proper deity. We are not satisfied with providing money and worldly goods to those in need; we also want them to organize their lives in ways we consider appropriate. We seem to be of the opinion that if we sustain them, this is not too much to ask; doing what we tell them is the price they pay for getting what they do.

Generous souls do not seem to realize that demanding something in return for what we offer converts the gift relationship into a commercial transaction. Instead of giving freely, with no strings attached, we buy suitable behavior with our contributions. In this way, the gift robs recipients of their freedom: donors believe they are owed not only thanks but also compliance. A gift properly understood imposes no obligation beyond heartfelt thanks; once the present is handed over, the giver surrenders control over the object without acquiring power over the recipient. In sending friends a present, I do not obtain the right to complain if they re-gift it, just as in giving money to beggars, I cannot demand that they invest it. Generosity is a costly virtue, requiring that we cede something of value without the expectation of any return.

There are, of course, cases in which help does not function as the price of control and yet the donor receives a benefit. Some individuals enjoy seeing their names on buildings in colleges;

others take delight in acquiring a reputation for generosity or in making others envy their wealth. Those who give anonymously may aim for the pleasure of secrecy or the sense that they deserve special credit for not wanting public accolades. Fellow feeling runs so strong in some humans that they take delight in the flourishing of life everywhere. Such splendid people give simply to see others do well in life; they assume the cost of college for promising young people, provide clean water by paying to drill wells in faraway lands, and send medical supplies to wherever they are needed.

The motives for helping others are varied and in many cases harmless. Often, though not always, only the results matter: so long as other people are benefited, it is unobjectionable for donors to derive a measure of good from their deeds. The one signal exception to this relates to control. Respect for liberty, which is respect for life, makes using aid to strip others of their decision-making power unacceptable. There are two important conditions that legitimate help must meet: whenever possible, it has to be temporary and not a move to take over other people's lives, and it must be offered on the recipient's own terms. These are tough requirements—the first because the people most likely to need help quickly get used to being taken care of, and the second because outsiders tend to think they know best what distressed people need. Help of the proper sort is therefore very difficult to provide. It requires that those seeking aid retain a proud independence and persons offering it refrain from acting as if they knew it all.

When they fall and scrape their hand, children solicit sympathy from their parents. The outpouring of love and kisses makes the pain go away but leaves happy memories of closeness and concern. After the dirt is washed away and the pain is long gone, the hand is offered again, as if hurting, for the same intense attention. If the action yields success, habits build easily and a sort of dependence develops. Even animals display this tendency. At one point we put out some leftovers for a couple of raccoons; the next night, they brought their friends and waited for the handout. Generally, when something desirable is free for the taking, intelligent creatures of all sorts avail themselves of it. This is as true of humans on the personal level as it is in relation to welfare payments by the government. Some people are perfectly content to become dependents and have others pay their way.

As early a source of insight into the human condition as the Bible makes it clear that labor is both necessary for the maintenance of life and thoroughly unpleasant. God's punishment for disobedience in the Garden of Eden was for humans to earn their living by the sweat of their brows—that is, by backbreaking labor. The only difference between those days and ours is that, for many, crushing boredom and being commanded about in their jobs have replaced heavy physical toil. As a result, with the exception of some devoted persons, mainly professionals, people are happy to avoid work. Lottery tickets represent the grand hope of being able to flourish without care and labor, as does the agreeable fiction of a forgotten maiden aunt leaving one a few million dollars.

The trouble is that people who are content to live off others blind themselves to the fact that what they graciously accept was earned by labor of the very sort they try to escape. What to them seems effortlessly available is, in the world as it exists after the Garden of Eden, anything but free. Parents have to stop what they are doing and use their time and energy to console their children. Food for raccoons was made by someone and bought by others who worked to be able to afford it. Welfare payments—in fact, anything given to anyone—require somebody's labor, so people who think that anything is free for the taking know only half of the story. Whether it requires money or effort, generosity has its cost. Consumption is impossible without production, and giving merely shifts the burden of that cost.

The famous British thinker John Locke viewed nature as the "commons" of humankind, a store of valuable resources from which all could take whatever they reasonably needed. The idea of moderation, of appropriating no more than we sensibly require, is importantly right, but supposing that what nature provides is free misses the mark. Locke himself did not believe it, reminding us that nature's bounty becomes our property only when we mix it with our labor. And indeed fish have to be caught, trees cut down, and gold mined, requiring activities that are by no means trivial or free. Viewed in one light, labor is the most costly of goods, almost sacred: as effort exerted, it is identical to human life itself. The time and energy expended on any activity can never be regained, so in offering our work we pledge an irretrievable portion of our limited days.

Humans have achieved a measure of control over nature through social cooperation. We work together to accomplish what no single individual could even imagine doing. We take care of the young and the old of the species, we subscribe to principles demanding kindness to strangers, and we engage in huge construction projects to benefit our communities. In better societies, though perhaps not in all, the sick receive care and the unfortunate aid. No other species on the planet shows the systematic caring and humane concern that seems natural to Homo sapiens.

Unfortunately, however, our social achievements obscure the personal costs of living in populous communities. These include the sense that because we earn our living in gigantic institutions, we cannot control our own lives. We feel ambushed by circumstance and manipulated by the people who work with us. We are ignorant of what our institutions accomplish or perpetrate partly by means of our acts, and therefore we refuse to assume responsibility for consequences to which we contribute. These costs of our comfortable lives are at last receiving some attention. What we have not noticed is the extent to which we become victims of our sympathy. Caring is an emotion greatly fostered by social life and may be one of the conditions of the success of our species. But it can be exploited, denying us the choice of how to dispose of our goods and money.

On the streets of many European cities, pregnant gypsy women, trailing dirty children in diapers, wail for help to ease their misery. They present themselves and their brood as desperately needy, thinking that good people will not let children starve. If the performance is believable, donations flood in: tourists are moved by seeing mother and children in evident distress. The scene captivates to such an extent that we fail to inquire if it is a show and, if it isn't, what business the woman had in bringing so many beggars into this cruel world. In one respect, of course, the woman's past decisions are irrelevant; all that counts is the present hunger and our goodwill, by means of which she holds us hostage and makes us give.

Something like this occurs with beggars everywhere and with people who are healthy and able to work yet live on government aid. Their own role in placing themselves in a desperate situation is beside the point when we behold their misery. Perhaps they never got parental care or an education; drug use might have dulled their minds; they may have developed bad habits and not many useful skills. All of this is regrettable and awful, but in the meantime they must have dinner and a place to sleep. We are rightly captured by the sight of need and cannot say even to ne'er-do-wells that the time has come to pay. This is how and why the morally reckless can exploit decent people and render themselves permanent dependents. They know the demand that they get jobs or an education is easily sabotaged; they don't have to comply because, so long as our society remains morally sensitive, all they have to do is show their penury.

Civilized countries have replaced the cruel neglect of earlier centuries with humane systems of aid. In the process, however, we have become prisoners of our goodwill, having lost the ability to say no to the plea for aid, even if it is exploitative. Liberation from this impotence, which is as bad for the recipient as it is for the donor, serves as the reason why, for the most part, helping others must be a temporary affair. Naturally we must make exceptions for people who are genuinely unable to take care of themselves: quadriplegics, those with severe mental problems, the very young and the very old, among others, must receive care through private charity or organized benevolence. The rest, however, must be made to understand that the aim of help is not to liberate them from their problems, but to provide instruments for dealing with them.

Establishing aid as a permanent requirement of life for people who could achieve operational independence invites others to take over decision making for them. This is a natural development that begins with setting conditions for the receipt of aid and ends with a near total loss of autonomy. Those who cannot or will not take care of themselves come to be viewed as in need of protection, which takes the form of denying them choice and the lessons of living. The process is reminiscent of dealing with children, whom we judge unable to make sound decisions or too tender for some experiences. The difference is that children can look forward to the time when they will be able to choose on their own, but adults who need constant help are permanently denied self-determination.

Not everyone understands why lifelong dependence is harmful to those who give, to those who receive, and to the society that creates and supports such exchanges. Donors rightly feel aggrieved that they work while others who lay claim to a part of their earnings may exert themselves only in search of a good time. They resent it when able-bodied people live off them and make no effort to get a job. It twists the soul to see that one is being used, and it embitters people when the supposed injustice of some enjoying riches while others remain poor is remedied by the injustice of having to share the fruits of labor with those who prefer not to work. The splendid sympathy humans have developed with the unfortunate stands in danger of eradication when the needy are seen as schemers unwilling to take care of themselves.

Long-term dependence is just as harmful to the recipients of organized charity as it is to the donors, but for other reasons. Since giving does not eliminate the disparity between the haves and the have-nots, some people supported by the community tend enviously to demand more. A comment emblematic of this attitude comes from a street person in New York, who is reported to have said that he would be glad to quit living in alcoves and subway stations if he were offered an apartment overlooking Central Park. A personal experience makes the same point more painfully. While walking near a church in Budapest, I was approached by an old woman asking for money. The torn clothes, the labored walk, and the history of suffering inscribed on her face made me reach into my pocket. I gave her what coins and paper money I found and wished her well. She counted the money at a glance, came closer, and spat on me for what she must have considered inadequate generosity.

Further, the readiness to make do with what can be got free in order to avoid the pain of work creates habits of inaction and, eventually, laziness. Youthful vigor and free time combine to beget children, addiction to drugs, and a taste for crime. Hosts of children grow up without role models or guidance and seek escape from desperation by leaving home to have children of their own. Since enough money to survive comes without the need to do anything, self-control and delayed gratification can be set aside; without them an education is impossible to attain, and without education there is no way to break the cycle of poverty.

A system of transfer payments to aid able-bodied but underskilled persons also hurts the society that institutes it. Individuals can make sound decisions about acquiring dependents. If they don't want children, they can take preemptive measures. They may decide to help another, less fortunate person or family by giving money or offering services. They can contribute to voluntary organized charity, such as community groups or churches that come to the aid of people facing ruin. All of these activities are freely chosen, and it is clearly understood that they have a time limit. No one is entitled to such help, and therefore no one can demand or expect to receive it indefinitely. As the spontaneous response of sympathy, it is meant to tide people over until they can get on their feet again. In taking food to a family that mourns a recent death, one is not signing on as their permanent, unpaid chef.

The situation is altogether different when a society establishes welfare payments as a matter of right. Original sin is supposed to be the wickedness that inheres in us not because of what we do, but because of who we are. The modern world has invented an original virtue that parallels original sin, declaring that we are worthy simply because we are human beings, and that status confers upon us unearned benefits. The Universal Declaration of Human Rights goes so far as to award paid vacations to all, simply because they belong to such an excellent species. The astonishing fact is that entitlements of this sort are instituted without regard to the nature of existence on this planet, supposing that the goods of life do not have to be created by labor and can therefore be distributed at will.

To view anything in life as an entitlement presents a lop-sided picture; it overlooks the effort necessary to provide what people think is their due. Precisely because nothing is free, the idea that some individuals are entitled to things and services that others must supply splits society into two camps: one that labors to create the necessities of life and another that spends its energy on demanding and consuming them. The inevitable result is mutual resentment that can lead to open conflict. Each group carries the banner of justice. Those who want a share of what others create demand a more even distribution of goods and money; working people insist on a more even level of contribution from everyone to the productive process. A society that fosters this conflict cannot be at peace with itself and faces constant political struggle focused on the scope and conditions of free benefits.

The need to support a growing class of people who consume without producing much and by paying no taxes fail to shoulder their share of social burdens sets neighbor against neighbor and impoverishes the community. In its attempt to be humane, the society contributes to the malformation of its members, teaching them by its actions that it is acceptable to live off the efforts of others. By being softhearted and generous, the community establishes the conditions of its self-destruction; it creates a permanent underclass that exerts political pressure for more entitlements and does not permit decision making on the basis of sound economic principles.

Let me stress that the generosity of liberal societies is an admirable moral trait. Human needs must be met and huge disparities of income represent a legitimate concern. Discrimination on the basis of race, gender, and religion has established subcultures where failure has become the norm, and even though in the past fifty years many doors to achievement have opened, the harmful effects of exclusion have not all been overcome.

But we cannot deal with such problems successfully by disregarding the tendency of human beings to take advantage of what is offered free of charge and their delight in avoiding labor. The Robin Hood principle of taking from the rich to give to the poor opens a Pandora's box of initiatives that are destined to fail and in the process to create pockets of permanent dependency. The way to combat poverty is by promoting the acquisition of valuable or at least useful skills and encouraging their vigorous use in work. Of course we must help those who need temporary help, are unable to work, or cannot develop new skills. The young, the old, the ill, and the disabled rightly demand our best efforts to aid them. We must not leave them alone; we can and must do everything for them once we have carefully separated them from those who want to game the system by getting paid for inactivity.

The difficulty of delivering help where it is truly needed and where it will not be abused is demonstrated by unemployment insurance. A system of such insurance is a genuinely humane response to need. As an act of appropriate kindness, caring communities rightly undertake to support individuals who lose their jobs. The aid is meant to be a temporary expedient, enabling people to meet their most urgent financial obligations until the next job comes along. Although it is a shining example of generosity, the system suffers from some effects that are defects.

A steady income, even if modest, tends to remove the urgency of finding new employment; recipients can take a break from labor and ask if the jobs available are worthy of their skills. Necessity no longer propels their actions, and they come to feel that they do not need to look for some job, but only for the right one. Paradoxically, the money that is meant to help people obtain new employment thus tends to reduce the motivation for work and results in increased or prolonged unemployment. We see here once again the way in which liberal society becomes the victim of its moral principles. Humane programs are easily exploited, subverting them to achieve results that are the opposite of what had been intended.

In tough economic times when jobs are not plentiful, the community thus faces unacceptable alternatives. Deciding not to extend unemployment benefits leaves people destitute and represents a violation of humane principles. Extending benefits, on the other hand, is counterproductive, leading to longer stretches of unemployment and a more distant end to recession. Some think that paying individuals when they do not work is in some sense of the word "socialist." This word has multiple meanings, but it is interesting to note that no less a social engineer than Joseph Stalin himself refused to attach any sentimental connotations to the term. Socialism, which he thought was a stage of society on the way to communism, operates on the principle that "he who does not work, neither shall he eat." This is at a cruel distance from the beliefs of liberal society, which would sooner be duped and exploited than cause or condone suffering.

The problem is that liberal societies focus on the immediate need of people seeking food stamps, unemployment benefits, or welfare payments. That need is real, but it must be placed in the broader context of its causes and of the likely outcome of honoring it generously. Since one of its primary sources is lack of marketable skills, the message must reach the schools that those who don't learn will have a difficult time making their way in the world. This is not quite Stalin's harsh message, because there is no actual starvation involved, only the threat of future suffering as a pedagogical device. If we imbued young people with the urgency of preparing for a life of work and thereby forestalled the growth of unproductive habits, we would see welfare rolls diminish over time and enable many more people to enjoy the satisfactions of self-reliance and achievement. For those who nevertheless develop habits of work avoidance and reliance on others, continued government aid could be made dependent on significant efforts at self-improvement.

The theme of leaving others alone can be used as a dark cloud menacing able habitual non-contributors to productive life. They need to understand that the community is prepared to educate them and to help them find jobs. But its largesse will come to an end, so finding work will soon acquire the urgency of supper. Being left to fend for themselves is an undesirable prospect for those who hope for lifetime support, although it serves as the ideal of productive people whose work is appreciated. The grand ideal of social justice is conceived in a one-sided fashion today: it is thought to involve helping those less well-off to gain access to the goods of life, but not aiding others to retain the goods they have earned through their talent and labor. In the name of social justice, governmental power separates successful people from a portion of their earnings in order to hand it to the nonworking needy. When the money goes to people George Bernard Shaw spoofed as "the undeserving poor," it is not surprising that workers who are forced to perform involuntary acts of charity come to view the ideal of social justice with growing suspicion. Is it, they ask, more than a pretense for providing a comfortable life for those who make little or no social contribution?

These comments may be read as amounting to a glorification of labor. Our society, imbued with the Protestant ethic, does indeed value work with nearly religious fervor. This leads to hurry, excessive stress, early heart attacks, and the inability to enjoy the moment. But a valid consideration underlies the

Protestant ethic: the world as we know it does not yield the necessities of life without sustained human effort. This is especially true in the temperate zone, where only timely and substantial intervention saves us from starving to death. Without labor, we would be exposed to the elements and perpetually hungry; all the benefits of civilized life would be denied us. Although there is something satisfying about seeing the world assume the shape of our will, there is nothing glorious about labor. Yet it is necessary and people can avoid it only by shifting its burden to others. This is inevitable and acceptable in the case of such groups of people as the very young, the very old, and the ill, but able-bodied individuals who refuse to expend the effort to sustain themselves make an unjust demand on others to support them.

The second major condition of helping people is that the aid be in accord with the needs and values of the recipient, not the donor. The natural temptation is to act on the opposite principle: we tend to suppose that people who need help are so poor at taking care of themselves that they cannot have a sound idea of what is good for them. This, in fact, is frequently not the case. Some people place themselves in situations where they need help precisely because they know what they want and pursue it relentlessly. The notion that all humans share the same values is a fiction and a hope. Achilles chose glory and an early death; how could we argue that he was wrong? We may find it difficult to understand his life and perhaps impossible to approve it, but the alternative of ruling a small, dusty kingdom for many years would have been worse than death for him. He knew what he wanted, and he needed help only to start a good war in which to go down in flames.

We find the same clarity of purpose and imperfect control of means in many less-distinguished individuals. Some alcoholics simply love to drink; they look not for the reorganization of their lives, but only for help in paying for the next libation. Gay people are not helped by matchmakers who introduce them to members of the opposite sex. Hungry vegetarians are not properly aided by offering them steaks and pork chops, and we do not improve the lot of hitchhikers who ask for a ride to New York by taking them to Seattle. The world is full of ignorant offers of assistance, many of them well meant and sincere, but genuinely unhelpful, nevertheless.

Generally, help consists in providing the means to ends established by others. Often, we make the assumption that we know the ends others want to attain or, even more boldly, that everyone answers to the same purposes. Such suppositions, reassuring as they are, enjoy no basis in fact. Human natures are astonishingly varied, and nowhere do their differences show themselves more strikingly than in what we treasure. The commitments of others can be as unintelligible as contradictions: I cannot imagine why anyone would want to be dean, or fat, or in love with an ugly woman. Yet I have to admit that many academics would see their dreams fulfilled if they could rise to administrative distinction; that hefty individuals enjoy the good-natured delights of excessive indulgence; and that people who strike me as hideous or deformed are viewed by others as blessed with uncommon beauty. Individuals die for causes that do not even rise to the attention of others or enact principles fit only for the criminally insane.

We are very different from one another, so any idea that we know what is proper for human beings everywhere and everywhen is presumptuous. We may know the norm in our society at a certain moment of its history, but even that momentary standard is riddled with exceptions and in the process of change. Therefore, we cannot argue from what uniformity we observe to the normative unity of a single, universal human nature. The local is often mistaken for the natural, and the natural is supposed to transcend the limitations of time. Those who believe this live a comfortable illusion at the cost of inability to see the rich diversity that surrounds them and the historical processes that gnaw away even at the most stable local equilibrium.

The idea that we know what is good specifically for this or that person, for friend or neighbor, is as baseless as the claim of insight into human nature in general. In spite of what many learned but inattentive thinkers maintain, there is an impenetrable privacy surrounding every person. Careful and extended observation can give others an idea of the character and values of people, but there is no assurance that what is revealed matches the secrets of the heart or, once made known, is not already in process of change. It is a mistake to believe loud protestations of commitment to conventional values; gays in the closet, uncaught spies, and cheating mates live double lives, making sure their public behavior does not reflect their deepest convictions. Even the family practices of one's neighbor can be baffling, and some spouses complain after thirty years of marriage that they live with a person they don't know.

Even if each private value has some corresponding public manifestation—a rather unlikely possibility—people tend to hide or disguise the revealing behavior. Many silent devotions and fervent cravings are never disclosed; we learn about them only from the diary of the departed or by bold conjecture on the basis of ambiguous evidence. Only private individuals are in a position to have direct knowledge of the experiences that vivify their lives; they alone recognize what occasions their despair and delight. They can, of course, tell others, revealing what they wish, but no matter how hard they try, they cannot convey the color, the feel, and the intensity of their inner lives. There is nothing mysterious about this privacy; we live it and feel surrounded by it every day. Unfortunately, when we are tempted to tell others how to live, we forget its implications and believe, for a moment, that we know their purposes.

Is it possible that even though we don't know the values by which people live, we grasp more clearly than they do the purposes that should move them? This is a claim not of insight into foreign psyches, but of understanding the world of human values. As such, it is a momentous conceit. Aristotle, Kant, and Mill were three of the greatest moral philosophers, and they could not agree on the way to lead or even to assess the moral life. Aristotle's virtue, Kant's duty, and Mill's search for pleasure represent alternative conceptions of what makes lives worthy. If they could not come to peace over ultimate values, is it likely that untrained, uncritical, and unreflective people will stumble on a clear conception of the final good? If we don't have a thorough knowledge of our neighbors, we definitely cannot establish ideals for them. The most likely candidates for such ideals derive from what we do and what pleases us. But our practices are unlikely to find favor with others, and imposing them is almost certain to be resisted.

Some people believe that helping others is not a matter of providing the means they need to attain their ends, but of clarifying for them—or with them—the purposes they should pursue. This job used to fall to priests and ministers and maiden aunts, but it has now been professionalized and handed to psychological counselors and "life coaches." In our fast-moving and relatively unguided society, more and more young people find the services of such individuals of significant value. As early as the days of Socrates, we knew that extended conversation can clear the mind. If the discourse goes on for too long, dependence is likely to develop and the decision-making capacity of people is compromised. But temporary measures to combat confusion, rehearse possibilities, and counteract aimlessness can generate wholesome results.

In such conversations, however, whether with professional psychologists or a helpful neighbor, everything depends on the approach of the counselor. The ideal is to serve as midwife to self-discovery, listening carefully and asking clarifying questions. The foundation of such relationships must be respect for the integrity of the persons being helped. It must be guided by the conviction that they and they alone can solve their problems. In this way, when we help others we still leave them alone, caringly—even lovingly—sharing their concerns but refusing to take over their lives by telling them what to value or what to do. Help of this sort strengthens our bonds in society because it promotes the power and the freedom of each to stand alone.

7

INDEPENDENCE AND THE ANTHILL

ANT COLONIES HAVE survived for millions of years by means of a rigid social structure favorable to the community but not to the individuals within. Necessary labor is divided in such a way that some ants serve as powerful soldiers while others forage and provide food for the community. A relatively small number are consigned to early deaths because of infections contracted in removing the colony's waste; if they want to change function or approach regular members of the society, they are summarily killed. Males live only to impregnate the queen; they die shortly thereafter. Minor ants, the smallest within the colony, move in battle like the Russian army in the First World War, swarming over the enemy and overwhelming it with their superior numbers. Old, ill, and crippled ants are assigned the job of protecting the colony's trails, sacrificing themselves, as needed, for the good of the whole.

If we pay attention to these tiny bits of life, we realize that ants are capable of stunning feats of daring and social cooperation. The principle underlying their success is the dispensability of nearly any individual member of the colony; they acknowledge no personal search for fulfillment and no right to life. The good of the community overshadows the claims of individuals, and members seem not to hesitate when called upon to make the ultimate sacrifice.

There have been, and there still are, human societies that resemble those of the ants, in which the dominant value is the survival of the whole. The armies of Attila the Hun and the hordes of Genghis Khan consisted of warriors who faced death daily and wanted little for themselves beyond momentary pleasure. The ethos of North Korea today appears similar to that of an ant colony united by devotion to its queen; cultic worship of the leader and unquestioning obedience to his edicts come close to a human equivalent of ant life. Even in more permissive human societies, there are analogues to the behavior of ants in a colony. People who exalt the glory of dying for country or for God and those who insist on the preeminent importance of doing one's duty endorse ant values at the expense of the individual search for meaning and satisfaction. Whoever speaks on behalf of social order defined in terms of selfless uniformity believes that humans would be better off seeking fulfillment in a greater whole and embracing universal values in place of a life of choice.

Moreover, historical developments may well force human communities in the direction of antlike rigidity. Vast increases in population require the establishment and enforcement of rules of interaction. To maintain order in hugely populous societies, it may become necessary to assign duties, jobs, or social roles to people and to control the trajectory of their lives. The avoidance of chaos is a mighty justification for imposing an order no one likes and yet none can countermand. That our children or grandchildren may live in an inhuman world that crushes variety and individual initiative is not science fiction, but a threateningly real possibility. In such a society, individual choice would be minimized and the good of the whole would invariably trump all deviant desires. People would not be left alone to live as they see fit, and all of us would feel called upon to make our neighbors do what society demands.

In addition to the growth of the population, at least three other factors favor the emergence of such antlike nations. The first is the possible exhaustion of the resources of the earth. Current economies are based on energy derived largely from coal and oil, which exist below ground in finite quantities. Iron ore, copper, and other metals necessary for our comfortable lives also are limited and require growing effort to obtain. To be sure, what counts as a resource is a matter of the technology available to utilize it. Oil wasn't a resource until we developed ways to convert it into usable commodities, such as gasoline, and invented the internal combustion engine. But the growth of technology is dependent on human inventiveness, and that, in turn, requires the transformative power of the imagination. Unfortunately the imagination is endangered whenever choice is denied. Innovation comes not as a result of government subsidies, where even the applications to obtain them demand a conventional cast of mind, but of mad private investments in ways of thinking that make new connections and turn accepted facts inside out. This suggests that the restriction of choice is a positive feedback loop; even a modest effort to control human life leads to the need for additional regulations.

The second and third developments are connected with the firmly held beliefs of liberal society. The conviction that human beings are entitled to have their needs met irrespective of their contribution to economic life exerts a harmful influence on the desire to work. Government programs that commendably relieve suffering by unemployment insurance payments, welfare distributions, and food stamps are easily converted into support without a deadline. Life sustained in this way is far from glorious, yet it tempts people who enjoy ample free time and could, in any case, not earn much more with heavy labor than they receive for staying home. In times of economic stress, the number of welfare recipients grows until as much as a third of the population lives off the labor of the rest and nearly half pays no taxes but votes for politicians willing to increase benefits. No nation can sustain such an unfavorable ratio of producers to consumers without facing economic collapse. At first only the well-to-do are struck with additional rules and taxes, but soon the middle class comes to feel the burden as well. When there is nothing more to give away, the society has to restore fiscal health by intrusive regulations that touch the lives of even the poorest people. The process is that of the gradual loss of choice and results in everyone being told, and eventually made, to do what others consider necessary.

Liberal society also believes that war is unnecessary; its horrors belong to the past and, fortunately, enlightened people no longer have to face them. This comfortable illusion rests on the assumptions that everyone values life, everyone is as rational as we believe ourselves to be, and everyone is willing to talk things out. The fact that such has never been the case in the history of humankind is not considered a valid objection to this optimism because, the believers in talk maintain, never before have people been as enlightened as they are today. Supposedly, all we have to do nowadays is to show good faith toward our enemies and the road will open to omnipotent conversation, which is certain to yield results satisfactory to both sides. The fact that members of many nations want Americans dead and that some of them are willing to blow themselves up to take a few of us with them is also no objection; such people have simply not been approached the right way and made to understand that their good and ours are identical. If only we could sit down with individuals who think they hate us and let the discussion go on for long enough, they would agree to a mutually satisfying bargain.

I am not sure what is more naïve about this position—the faith in the power of talk or the expectation that people are prepared to surrender their deepest values. There may come a time when war will seem a childhood disease of humankind, but that time has not arrived. People who want to trim the defense budget to use the money for tackling social problems are likely to leave the country inadequately defended. It should not be difficult to understand that, unfortunately, we have implacable foes who tend to view those who do not deal with them on the basis of power as weak and easily manipulated. For this reason, negotiations can succeed only if they serve as the alternative to the application of force, and military power constitutes a credible threat only if there is a will to apply it. Liberal societies tend to lack the will to fight; when this becomes clear to warlike or totalitarian regimes, they can wring stunning concessions from their peaceful neighbors. Democracies engage aggressive countries on the battlefield only upon being attacked or when demands on them become intolerably excessive. Often this is tragically late, because by then aggressors are powerful enough to be difficult to defeat. At that point the mobilization of the resources of a liberal democracy requires extensive constraints and controls, converting the society into something close to an anthill. Here, once again, we see reenactment of the insignificance of individuals, the limitations of choice, and the mindless adherence to duty.

There is an ultimate nightmare scenario according to which in the future nearly all human freedom may be lost. The development of technologies of brain and behavior control is making it possible for experts to attain a previously unimaginable level of power over what others think and do. Carefully administered chemicals, deep brain stimulation, and certain forms of mind control can bring about actions desired by specialists or a central authority. The behavior is caused by the intervention of others, yet the people whose brains are manipulated believe that what they do is the outcome of their own decisions. We can see less extreme versions of this phenomenon among people who are easily influenced or given to imitation: they follow what others do but think their actions are shaped by their own ideas. Chemically achieved conviction is more assured, more swift, and more unquestioning than these, and once the drugs and manipulative procedures are fully developed, it renders people both docile and satisfied in their supposed self-determination.

The nightmare consists of precisely this conjunction of the lack of freedom and the false belief that we are masters of our thoughts and fate. To be satisfied as manikins and not to see the horror of being in someone else's power is repulsive to us today. But the inhabitants of an awful future may not know that they lack self-determination or may not even care that others control their every move. They may want nothing more than mindless grins, and embrace whatever impulse moves them as their own. The very contrast of freedom and external control may not make sense to them, either because they view it as insignificant if measured against their comfort or because the source of their restricted lives is carefully disguised. In either case, they will never taste the joy of free decision and hence fail to learn that happiness achieved is better than passive pleasure.

Such a sad world may never come about. We can draw comfort from the fact that for thousands of years the desire to be left alone—which is the hunger for freedom—has reasserted itself in small acts of defiance and momentous revolutions. Elimination of external control has served as a mighty ideal for which people were ready to give their lives. The ultimate danger to liberty is not cruel repression; sooner or later brave sacrifice defeats the controlling power. The history of humankind shows that alien domination can be broken; oppressors tend to be crushed; and dictators, along with their statues, are toppled in the city square. But what happens to freedom if dependence enters the heart and we become ants voluntarily? The need for order in a crowded world may leave the next generation, or the generation after that, with the sense that external direction is beneficial and freedom creates only chaos. Worse, they may come to think that liberty is attainable only by following regulations and that the desire to be left alone is an antisocial impulse.

If this is what our grandchildren will believe, we will not recognize ourselves in them. They may view the great American revolution as an unjustified social disturbance and seek the direction of experts in arranging even the minute details of their lives. They may come to believe that doing their duty is the purest pleasure and learn to appreciate each act forced out of them by external influence as one of their own. They may see self-determination as the ultimate expression of insecurity and self-reliance as a response to turbulent times. Perhaps they will not consider individuality as of much value and will not be tortured, as ants surely are not, by the meaning of their lives and by the prospect of death. We can see a few such perfectly integrated persons in our midst already, finding a happy life in hierarchical institutions with bishop or sergeant determining their daily rounds. But such self-surrender does not evoke admiration, and if our grandchildren turn in this direction, they will provide reason only for grief.

Sadness over these possible worlds aside, we must answer those lovers of community who believe that ant values may not be so bad after all. The desire for friends and a safe home is completely understandable: we need trusted companions and could probably not live well without them. But, unlike ants, humans have a self-image and enjoy extensive and deep relationships to themselves. They understand that they are the centers of their worlds, and they ask questions about the value of what they do. They live in private intimacy with themselves and believe that, worthy as self-sacrifice may be, its price is the annihilation of the person. The citizens of liberal states tend not to be religious, so they cannot look ahead to a time when good behavior earns heavenly rewards. They know, or think they know, that we have but one life and that surrendering it forces on us a finality unmatched by anything in our experience. They also know the well of emotion out of which the demand for independence rises, along with the need, probably biological, for operational self-determination.

Furthermore, the denial of choice is a grating experience; it is not a onetime event but causes anger and annoyance daily. The discomfort grows in proportion to the experienced difference between what is coerced and what is undertaken freely. The contrast is unavoidably present for everyone, because external influence has never succeeded in controlling every aspect of people's lives. Job descriptions and assignments of duty are presented in general terms, leaving ample room for individual decisions about how to comply. Even direct manipulation of the brain falls short of controlling every movement and every moment of life. That external force cannot govern all is clear in the military. Its rigid and extensive rules do not cover how soldiers are to use the latrine, and the pleasure of freedom there makes for a delicious contrast with what the sergeant demands at the end of the break.

Individual decision making is closely connected to creativity not because all choices are excellent, but because they constitute a broad field out of which the best responses can emerge. If we wished to establish a connection to Darwinian ideas, we could say that the wide spectrum of decisions is similar to the field of the spontaneous variations of living things from which the pressure of natural selection preserves only the most apt. Without such experimental structures and behaviors, responses remain stagnant and life sinks under the weight of institutionalized routine. Freedom multiplies actions and ideas, some of which turn out to be brilliant and others fundamentally flawed. The important fact, however, is that few if any of them could have occurred under conditions of enforced conformity. To leave people alone with their projects is to permit—even to encourage—the exercise of their private imaginations. The individual mind is the smithy that fashions tools and thoughts; liberating it so that it may work unencumbered is an investment in novelty.

Even the way humans honor their duty is superior to how ants perform their tasks. The response of the ant colony to what must be done is invariant and mechanical and stands in sharp contrast to the thoughtful and questioning approach of which humans are capable. Ants stand guard and attack intruders without reflection or hesitation. We do not know if they have an internal life, but to all appearances chemical stimuli are decisive in triggering their responses. We find instances of similar unthinking bravery among humans, but that is neither the norm nor what garners the highest praise. The person who, forgetting that he never learned to swim, jumps in a water-filled quarry to save a drowning child and consequently drowns is not the ideal of the human devoted to duty. We value questioning or at least an intelligent assessment of the situation prior to action. We admire people who actively commit themselves to causes, but not if their allegiance is automatic or lacks reasons to support it. We choose to do our duty instead of finding ourselves doing things that seem urgent though we don't know why.

Freedom is also closely connected to what many believe is the preeminent good in the universe. John Stuart Mill maintains that the greatest creation of humankind is humanity itself and that in the form of mature individuals, the human race constitutes the highest value. He rightly praises the harmonious development of all our faculties, seeing it as analogous to the growth of magnificent trees. And in fact there is something marvelous about the flowering of a person or a mind and something inspiring as we learn to appreciate the internal qualities and external achievements that require the integrated labor of the entire being. A community made up of such individuals would be like a mountain meadow, displaying a wondrous variety of flowers pleasing to the painter's eyes but lacking the systematic organization demanded by bureaucrats. We cannot, of course, rely on natural adjustments to be sure individuals don't get in each others' way; we must ensure that they don't harm one another in the process of their self-development. But the negative admonition that people cause each other no harm is very different and vastly less oppressive than the positive demand that they let others chart their course for them or that they fall in line with a uniform ideal.

In sum, then, the cost of making human communities approximate the self-sacrificial life of an ant colony is far too high. The loss of freedom and choice, of creativity and private decision making turns humans into mechanical appendages of a survival machine. Ants have managed to endure for millions of years, but, unlike humans, they have not improved their colonies, extended their lifespan, or bettered the quality of their existence. If our aim were restricted to the survival of our communities, individual inventiveness would receive no support and persons would enjoy only instrumental value. Questioning and free concern for the good of others, the two most useful and most admirable features of human character, would be altogether absent. Unless we blanked out our minds, we would live in perpetual frustration at having to do what we never chose. Ant values may be perfect for ant colonies; they would be a living nightmare for human beings.

Humans living together as flowers do in a field is a mighty but difficult ideal. How can we create such magnificent meadows? Can there ever be a community of individuals in which members are helped when in need but for the rest of the time are left alone to lead their lives, alone or with their chosen friends, as they see fit? There is no doubt that the odds are long that such an ideal world could ever come into existence and sustain itself. The meddlesome tendency of humans militates against it, as do the pleasures of crushing alien wills and making others do things without our having to bear the consequences. Claiming that these troublesome tendencies derive from human nature may be too easy; when we find it difficult or undesirable to make changes in what we do, it is a timeworn strategy to bless current practices as expressions of our unalterable constitution. There is not much in the world that cannot be changed or that will not change with time on its own. Even if we cannot achieve the ideal, we can move some distance in its direction by thoughtful and concentrated effort. We can increase freedom and improve life if we set our minds to modifying some of our habits and institutions.

The changes must begin with the aims and methods of raising children. Some parents consider their offspring sources of nuisance and misery and show little interest in contributing to their education. It is unfortunate that people like this burden themselves with children at all; it would be best for them to understand that not everyone needs to be a parent, at least in part because being one imposes stringent obligations. Most parents take their responsibilities seriously but make the mistake of thinking that young people are like computers that must be programmed to make the right responses. Such an attitude may create children who are obedient mechanisms for a while, delighting their parents by enacting what they were taught. But the teenage years bring rebellions that reject external influence and leave young people to face the complexities of the world with inadequate resources. The trouble comes from parents who insist on routine, and often on outmoded, responses instead of intelligent choice; they want to replicate themselves rather than prepare their children to make their own decisions in the difficult situations of life.

People who love freedom respect it at every age. Children value choice early in life and are capable of making intelligent decisions about a range of issues by the time they are two years old. What they want to wear, where they want to go, and how they want to play are clearly within their competence to determine, and thoughtful parents allow their decisions, even if inconvenient, to stand. Choice is one of many activities that can be learned only by doing; parents teach their children how to be free by allowing them the greatest possible level of safe operational independence. Young people, along with the rest of us, are apt to make a host of bad decisions, and parents are supposed to protect them from harmful consequences. But to nullify the outcomes of choice is to deny people their education. We have no incentive to avoid acts whose painful costs never come to haunt us. This means that parents have to be inventive and find ways to let the mistake hurt, yet protect the child from self-destructive actions.

I mentioned before that young children are fascinated by electric stoves whose heating elements turn red hot when set on High. They want to touch, perhaps even carry away or hug, the dangerous objects. They perceive the monition that doing so is not allowed as an alien order limiting their freedom. To avoid harm and maximize choice, parents can let their children rest their hands on the heating element when it is cold and then turn it on. As it heats, the children quickly remove their hands, understanding in an instant and without significant damage that the attractive is not always good. Similar strategies can be employed in other contexts to make room for choice, permit young people to learn by their experiments, and yet protect them from disastrous mistakes. It is well known that orders backed by threats and beatings simply do not work, yet many parents persist in commanding their children about, expecting them to bend even to absurd demands. What the parents forget is that in the long run their might dissipates and their children are left with fear, anger, and resentment. Family relations built on the exercise of power dissolve the bonds of love and display parents not as nurturing adults, but as demanding strangers. The key is to help the young grow sound, life-affirming habits, which is done best by guiding their development rather than forcing them into a mold prepared by others.

In high school, if not before, students are likely to experiment with sex and drugs, partly because of the pleasures they provide and partly because they are forbidden. Here, too, intelligence provides better guidance than do threats and power. Parenting is a partnership that aims to help children flourish. This requires, first and foremost, elimination of the negativity that denounces everything of interest to the young as dangerous, inappropriate, or wrong. If it is supportive, the partnership gives parents a say in ultimate decisions and enables them to voice the caution and need for self-control that they themselves learned through long experience. Forthright disclosure of personal failures often enables parents to gain the attention of their children and perhaps even a measure of influence over what they propose to do. Blanket prohibitions crush liberty and engender rebellion, so it may be best if proposed actions are represented as leading to undesirable outcomes rather than as violations of a sacred rule. The point throughout is not that the proposed actions will hurt the parents or the reputation of the family, but that they will harm the future of the young.

And indeed drugs and sex out of control amount to a major assault on unsuspecting experimenters, and the job of parents remains, as it has always been, to introduce hesitation into the heat of action and serve as the loving voice of reason. The readiness to undertake this task presupposes commitment to the freedom of the young, or else rejection of advice makes the advisor feel spurned. Love wants the good of the other as the other sees it; for this reason it has to be, as the Bible says, patient and even long-suffering. The deepest caring, therefore, involves freedom on at least two levels: the person who loves must display a steady commitment, and the individual loved must be accepted as an independent agent. Love that crowds, suffocates, or converts the other into an appendage of the self is not worthy of the name. We may enjoy possession of such tools and delight in seeing replicas of ourselves all over the world, but these are not proper objects of caring. Love is a relation between independent agents that is built on mutual respect and leaves the integrity of each untouched.

In some cases young adults learn to exploit their parents, viewing them as no more than useful tools for accomplishing what they want. This amounts to withdrawal from the partnership and often leads to bitter charges and sad recriminations. The emotional intensity of the clashes can be toned down by remembering that all the parties involved are independent agents entitled to make their own decisions. In cases of extreme aggression or wanton destructiveness, parents are justified in terminating their support of the young, just as the young are entitled to move out and try to make a life on their own. But respect for the liberty of young people requires that the impending break be presented as a choice. Even though money and social standing provide parents with greater power than their children can summon, it is important not to use that advantage to threaten or humiliate. Instead, parents can explain that their continuing support comes at a price and that its termination will likely entail significant consequences. A calm account of the alternatives moves the parties beyond guilt and vituperation and honors young people with trust in their decision-making capacity.

The freedom of individuals and general acceptance of it tend to level the playing field and place the might of choice in the hands of everyone. Unavoidable asymmetries of power continue to beset us: money, connections, natural endowments, and luck put some people in a better position than others. In the past few hundred years we have taken giant steps in the direction of eliminating these mostly undeserved advantages, but neutralizing all of them remains an idle dream. Not everyone can be a millionaire's child, and charm and grace are not easily taught. But we can insist on equalizing power at least in voluntary relationships, such as marriage. Since married partners are independent agents who freely choose to share their goods and lives, neither can exercise dominion over the other. A responsible husbanding (and "wifing") of resources must be assumed, and neither partner can demand an accounting from the other. The flow of information must remain unimpeded between the partners, and the initial assumption about contested issues must always be that the others in the relationship are rational agents who had good reasons for thinking and doing what they did.

Independence acquires special significance in old age precisely because it is endangered. For more than a hundred years the automobile has served as the instrument and symbol of independent agency. Aging robs us of the freedom a car in the garage represents to go where we wish whenever the spirit moves us. Soon we lose the ability to negotiate steps safely and eventually cannot even walk into the doctor's office. The ruin of our mobility is accompanied by the deterioration of mental functions: memories fade, reasoning slows, and decisions are framed in hesitation. Ultimately others have to assume our care and make decisions on our behalf; we forfeit control over both how we live and when we die. The aging of the population in industrialized countries makes it imperative that we face the problems associated with this awful decline, yet we seem not to want to see the predicament of the old from their standpoint. The wishes of the aging are routinely overridden, their decisions are "interpreted" to favor outcomes at odds with their intentions and their earnest desire to be done with existence is crushed in the name of the state's interest in sustaining life.

To respect people as free decision makers is to honor their decisions in matters both trivial and momentous. John Stuart Mill, a great champion of liberty, erred in his view of suicide, falling prey to the spurious argument that since killing oneself is irreversible, the state must not allow it. In reality, every decision and act is irreversible: although one may be able to divorce one's first husband, that remedy does not reverse the error of having married him. People who kill themselves cannot be summoned back from the grave, but nor can anything we do once it has happened. The young and those in the prime of life seem unable to understand why old people want to die, but that shows only that their experience is limited and that they cannot imagine a life without hope of improvement in a nursing home. With purposes fulfilled, and drained of energy, individuals can rightly feel that they are ready to go. The state should have no say in this; even beloved others can only plead for more time and testify to the loss they will feel. The danger is that the decision will come too soon, but even then there is room only for conversation, not for forceful intrusion. The last word about our future must be reserved for ourselves; as the crowning affirmation of our freedom, our decision to live or die must not be contravened.

Often we see bitter conflicts between the old and those designated to make decisions for them. The tendency is to infantilize the aged, countermanding their orders and mocking their pigheadedness in whispers behind their backs. Young children may not grasp how thoroughly they are at the mercy of adults; the life of the old becomes suffocating precisely because they see the impotence of their decisions and the death of their freedom. People who take over the lives of their parents need to remember that soon, too soon, their children will follow the pattern and do the same to them. Fellow feeling and self-defense demand that they honor the wishes of the old, granting them the widest possible range of self-determination. The argument that overturning their plans is meant to promote their good simply doesn't hold, because no element of their good is more central than their liberty. Except in cases of gross mental incompetence, no matter how difficult it is to be the instrument of intentions one rejects, we must let the decisions of the old prevail.

Collaboration in complex tasks is not spontaneous, so it must be governed by some central authority. Work, accordingly, inevitably entails at least a partial surrender of freedom; people hired to keep books cannot indulge their fancy and spend their days playing the accordion. The question is how far employers can and ought to go in defining the details of what they expect from their workers. If a ditch needs to be dug, it is sensible to explain where and of what dimensions, but there is no need to insist that in the process shovels be held at a certain angle. Similarly, salesmen must be told which items in inventory need most to be pushed out the door, but employers should not demand control over their workers' sales techniques. Assembly line–like conditions, where every action is carefully choreo-graphed, and handbooks with elaborate job descriptions tend to rob workers of spontaneity and serve to demoralize them. Here, again, leaving as much room as possible for freedom yields excellent results. If management explains the ends to be attained, workers can often find the most expeditious means. Those closest to the execution of plans are the most likely to know shortcuts and pitfalls; their inventiveness far exceeds that of the efficiency experts who visit for a day.

Letting workers determine some of what they do and much of how, provides a host of incidental benefits. It makes them into partners in the enterprise, enabling them to appropriate the tasks they perform as their own. The deadly tedium of endless repetition is replaced by novel challenges that fall to workers to resolve. Most important perhaps, employees experience a sense of freedom or self-possession that makes their work pleasur-able. The feeling of compulsion, of what Marxists call "forced labor," disappears, and workers are invited—as in what started as Japanese quality circles—to share in the exhilaration of solv-ing problems. This underscores the fact that, contrary to what Marx believed, the de-alienation of labor occurs not as a result of communal ownership of the means of production. Whether the state or the faceless "people" own everything makes little difference so long as work operates by rigid rules that are be-yond the control of individuals.

If we want to live together as flowers in a field, last but not least we must reconceive the nature and role of legislation. We need protection from others in our community and from exter-nal forces. In a populous world there must also be some rules of interaction in relation to driving, commercial transactions, and the security of person and property, among others. Requiring that we drive on the right side of the road is an understandable and necessary restriction of freedom, as are laws proscribing fraud and extortion. But government officials and legislators seem to believe that assuring the opportunity to engage in the pursuit of happiness is not enough; they wish to protect us from the consequences of our actions and thereby *provide* our share of happiness. Laws governing the availability of drugs, the sale of organs, and the purchase of health insurance are not designed to protect individuals from one another; their function is to make sure people don't commit what bureaucrats consider errors of choice and always have available to them what are thought to be the essential conditions of happiness.

We have already seen the pervasive mistakes of this mode of thought. People resent others engineering their satisfaction; forcing actions on individuals in the name of their happiness renders them unhappy. The wide variety of human natures makes it clear that there are no universal conditions of fulfillment. Moreover, no external observers can know with certainty what is of value to an individual, and even if they did, they would have no basis for judging it wrong. The point is not that people are always right in their choices—even God did not eliminate bad decisions in the Garden of Eden—but that our operational independence and the intimacy we enjoy with ourselves put us in a privileged position when it comes to knowing what we want. And as adults, even if we make mistakes, we must not be protected from the consequences of our actions.

Sound legislation must take these considerations into account. No matter how attractive it may be to promote the general welfare by making people do all manner of things they would rather not, there are some matters concerning which no laws should be passed. The proper business of government does not include intrusion into the private lives of citizens so long as they do not represent threats to one another. It should stay out of the business of telling people what to value, whom to worship, and how to pursue their happiness. Passing laws banning incandescent light bulbs, slow-flushing commodes, and top-loaded washing machines makes legislators look as absurd as they in fact are. To combat this perception, they must learn to believe that leaving others alone is a fundamental virtue and that the resultant freedom is a central part of the public good. This means that in a number of cases more is accomplished by doing nothing than by passing laws. Under any circumstances, before voting on a bill, legislators should explore its cost in liberty.

Putting regulations in place is much easier than taking them off the books. If we keep this simple fact in mind, we will be less likely to rush to legislative solutions than we are today. We will be especially cautious about bills of inordinate complexity and those offered at a time of panic or politically motivated haste. It is particularly important that lawmakers actually read the bills they vote on instead of listening to the advice of staff or following party directives. The recent record of legislators in this regard has been nothing short of dismal. The cruel irony of extolling the benefits of freedom while subscribing to its uncontrolled and poorly understood limitation obviously escapes their ken.

People have often remarked that those who lack liberty are the most in love with it. This, unfortunately, is true. Individuals living under tyrannical rule are willing to sacrifice their lives to assure that they and their families are able to choose what they want without external intervention. The honor roll of those who died for liberty transcends national and all other bounds. The cruel bite of not being left alone to lead one's life as one sees fit begins to be felt only when central authority or nameless others attempt to wrest control of one's existence. Those who enjoy the blessings of liberty tend to forget how quickly self-reliance can be stripped from them and how easily an oppressive government or a collection of busybodies can make life a nightmare for individuals. It is essential to remember that freedom is ever in danger. May there always be brave people who resist meddling and are willing to die for the right to be left alone. And may their sacrifice always be crowned with success.

JOHN LACHS is Centennial Professor of Philosophy at Vanderbilt University. He is author of *Stoic Pragmatism* (Indiana University Press, 2012), *A Community of Individuals,* and *In Love with Life.*

CPSIA information can be obtained at www.ICGtesting.com
Printed in the USA
BVOW05s0317151014

370705BV00040B/125/P